Basic Soccer Skills

For Kids

Chest Dugger

Table Of Contents

Free Gift Included

As part of our dedication to help you succeed in your career, we have sent you a free soccer drills worksheet. This is the "Soccer Training Work Sheet" drill sheet. This is a list of drills that you can use to improve your game; as well as a methodology to track your performance on these drills on a day-to-day basis. We want to get you to the next level.

Click on the link below to get your free drills worksheet.

https://soccertrainingabiprod.gr8.com/

ABOUT THE AUTHOR

Chest Dugger is a pen name for our soccer coaching brand, Abiprod. We provide high quality soccer coaching tips, drills, fitness and mentality tips to ensure your success.

We have been fans of the beautiful game for decades. Like every soccer fan around the globe, we watch and play the beautiful game as much as we can. Whether we're fans of Manchester United, Real Madrid, Arsenal or LA Galaxy; we share a common love for the beautiful game.

Through our experiences, we've noticed that there's very little information for the common soccer fan who wants to escalate his game to the next level. Or get their kids started on the way. Too much of the information on the web and outside is too basic.

Being passionate about the game, we want to get the message across to as many people as possible. Through our soccer coaching blog, books and products; we aim to bring high quality soccer coaching to the world. Anyone who's passionate about the beautiful game can use our tactics and strategies.

DISCLAIMER

Introduction – What Kind of Skills are Important to Develop First?

Soccer is the most popular team sport in the world. It is perfect for kids to play. It is safe, simple and the skills required can be easily acquired. Becoming an expert player requires high levels of dedication, natural athleticism and innate skills. Any girl or boy can take to the sport and find enjoyment at their own level.

It is for this reason that the game is escalating to such a rapid extent in the US. And it is why the need for coaches and players is growing continuously and rapidly. After all, who would not turn down the chance for their kids to keep physically fit, to allow their natural competitiveness to be channeled in an organized way, to be kept busy in a manner that is both productive and worthwhile? In addition to this, soccer develops dexterity, problem solving, collaboration, friendship, respect, self-discipline, team spirit and sportsmanship. All of which are life skills that are best acquired young.

But there is so much to learn for youngsters who wish to become soccer players at a good club level. Shooting, defending, pressing, passing, controlling the ball, the laws of the game (even professionals struggle at times with the offside law as do, it sometimes seems, the referees themselves). And more important than all of these, children must learn about the spirit of soccer. Fair play and the sportsmanship mentioned above. This is especially so for today's youngsters facing all the pressures of growing up in a challenging world driven by the twin pressures of consumerism and social media.

This book will provide advice and tips for coaches and parents as they seek to help young people to become successful players. It will also help them to define 'success', whether that means spending a couple of hours per week with mates keeping physically fit in a fun environment, or moving through the academy levels and perhaps even achieving the ultimate goal of becoming a professional. The book includes numerous drills, key skills and a look at how child development affects young participants' progress as players. As such, it is essential reading for the would be coach, or the parent whose child is looking to start playing the game for a team. It offers new ideas for experienced coaches, with drills that can be adapted to the needs of players and teams.

We look in detail at offensive and defensive plays. We consider the basics of control. We look at dribbling skills, the mental side of the game and have a special chapter for parents.

We also look at the considerable benefits TV coverage can give to young players in promoting their enthusiasm for the game while allowing them to learn from the game's greatest exponents.

Most of all, we emphasize the importance of having fun. Suggested drills are enjoyable, the benefits of match play are stressed. Sometimes, soccer can become a little too serious (and what, in life, doesn't sometimes fall into that trap?). Coaches and officials within the game, with the best of intentions, forget that the young participants of the sport are just that. Young. It is all very well focusing planned development on future national teams, but a negligible percentage of participants will ever come even close to playing at that level.

What is most important about soccer is that all players enjoy it. Would the young Neymar or Hazard have become the player they are today if soccer training had been an unenjoyable chore? Almost certainly not.

And what children love most of all is to run, to shoot, to celebrate and to compete. (Note: not always to win, that is a much more adult perspective. Children who hate to lose learn that attribute from the adults around them. Winning is fine, but so is losing, especially if we gain from the experience.)

Provided we create the chances for young players to enjoy their soccer, becoming better people in the process, we will have happy children on our hands. Who could ask for more?

Basic Control Skills

Spain v England. The newly inaugurated Nations' Cup. It is a match that England must win but the odds are stacked against them. Possession is won deep in the English half and the ball is hit early and long.

It is not the best tactic, particularly against a well organised defense who have not overcommitted forward. Spain have kept two defenders back to deal with the threat of England's lone striker, Harry Kane. Kane has been on a good run of form, he won the Golden Boot at the World Cup, and is recognised as one of the best Number 9s in the world. But here he is isolated.

There is a touch of good fortune about the first stage of his work. As he heads towards goal, heavily marked and with the ball dropping, it catches the back of his foot. But from there, Kane's work is excellent. Aware that he is danger of losing the ball, he turns quickly, and gets into position. His first proper touch takes the ball away from his defenders, but does not remove all forward movement the attack. The second is sufficient to draw in a defender and create some space in behind him.

His control of the ball has also allowed another team mate to race forward in support. Kane's third touch is a beautifully weighted pass which brings that team mate into play and it takes just one further touch for the ball to be in the back of the net. All made possible because a hopeful pass forward was controlled with technical excellence and vision.

Control of the ball is key in soccer. Scouts look for that skill above all others when they are assessing the promise a young player might possess. It is the attribute that leads to quality passing, shooting and dribbling.

There are a number of stages to controlling the ball, all are important and while practising them might not be quite as much fun as shooting or dribbling, time spent on each aspect will deliver significant rewards.

Checking For Pressure

The precise method of gaining control depends, to some extent, on how much time the receiver has before they are tackled. Equally, a sharp decision has to be made as to whether the receiver moves towards the ball, remains in the same spot or moves away from the ball. As a general rule, it is best to move towards the ball, and this is a good default position to adopt. However, it is not always the strongest option.

Let us look at the information that a player needs to process to make their decision.

Move Towards the Ball: Usually, this will maximise time on the ball, taking pressure away from the first touch, which we will look at later in this chapter. It also reduces the chance of a pass being intercepted by the opposition, and allows the ball to be moved on quickly. Pace in an attack is often key to creating chances and scoring goals. The decision to move forward and towards the ball will be decided by the following factors:

- Is there a risk of interception?
- Will I have more time on the ball if I move towards it?
- Can I see a pass which will be made more quickly if I move to the ball?
- Am I unsure whether there are opponents nearby?

***Top Tip** – younger children often want to dribble rather than pass. This is their state of emotional development, where the 'id' is dominant. Set up a race, them against the ball. This way they see that the ball travels faster than they can run.*

Wait for the Ball: This is the decision to make when the intention is to take the ball, and drive forwards with a dribble, or a pass which continues to switch play. (By 'switching play' we mean moving the ball quickly from one side of the pitch to another, usually with no more than two or three passes). Players will decide whether to take a touch, or if the angle and pace of the pass is correct, and they have time, let it roll on and drive forward with a dribble or first time pass.

- Do I have time?
- Will moving towards the ball restrict the options I have when I take control of it?

Moving Away from the Ball: This is the least common option, but can be used when the pass is a long one, and position needs to change to control the ball most easily.

- Will the pass bounce in front of me, go over my head, or go past me before I can reach it?
- Is it a long pass which I will flick on with my head?

Making such decisions becomes second nature with practice, but two sets of drills can be used to help develop that instinct. The drills should aim to make the manoeuvres instinctive. One involves a simple look over the shoulder as the ball is played in, the second is a little more technical, and seeks to develop peripheral vision. The better this is, the less time the player spends with his eyes off the ball.

Control Drill – The Glance

In this drill, and each of the following where diagrams are presented, we use the following key:

- White circle – Predominantly offensive team;
- Black circle – Predominantly defensive team;
- Small grey circle – Ball;
- Thick white arrow – Movement of the ball;
- Narrow black arrow – Movement of offensive players;
- Thick black arrow – Movement of defensive players;
- Box – Grid, not to scale.
- Grey ovals (various sizes) – Additional goals, cones etc.
- We have used diagrams where we feel that a pictorial guide makes the drill clearer. Others are extremely straightforward (but no less effective for this) and can be communicated better through just words.

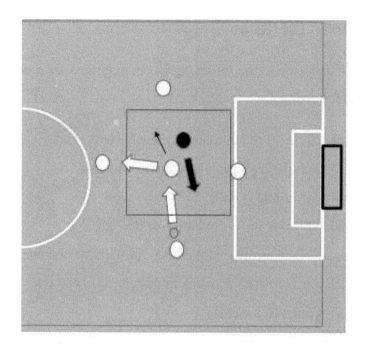

In 'The Glance' a simple 10 x 10 m grid is set up. There are five offensive players and one defensive. As skills improve, a second defensive player can be added. The drill is about improving players' awareness of the time they have. The ball is played into the offensive player in the grid, who can take two touches to lay the ball off to a team mate, and then move away from the defensive player. The ball is then played back in and the drill continues.

The central offensive player must glance around as the ball is played in, just a quick look. This will tell him or her the movement of the defensive player. This player's role is not to make a tackle, but to intercept where the next pass will go.

Control Drill – Developing Peripheral Vision

A fun, popular drill which is not directly linked to soccer. Sometimes, the game is called bulldog. The drill works particularly well indoors, but can be played outside. Two teams are organised. A narrow pitch is created, around 6 m x 20 m. The drill works best with a large group of players, but the pitch can be reduced in size if the numbers of players available is small.

One team lines up either side of the pitch (or, if indoors, one side can be the wall, which adds the further challenge of rebounds.) They are armed with a large number of light rubber or sponge balls. Team two must get from one end of the pitch to the other without being struck by one of the sponge balls.

Once hit they join the 'throwing' team. The game continues until there is a winner – the last 'untouched' player. The teams then swap around.

Seeing the Bigger Picture

Once players automatically decide on where to position themselves to receive the ball the next step is getting our youthful team to see the bigger picture. Although it is described here as a separate skill, in reality, deciding what to do with the ball happens almost simultaneously with deciding whether to wait or move towards or away from the pass.

The main priority is keeping possession, which is achieved with decisions above. Next is what to do once possession is maintained, and that is a much bigger decision which influences a number of subsequent decisions. Where to receive the ball, which body position to adopt and with which part of the body to control the ball are all matters which are selected following the decision of where the ball will go next.

Without wishing to get too much into child development, it is important to understand how children perceive the world. Until around the ages of five to six, this is completely from their perspective. Thus to try to get them to decide whether it is best to pass the ball, dribble it or clear it is pretty much impossible for this age. That is because they see the game only from their perspective, not that of the team. Much better with this age to work on skills.

As children get older, they do see the benefits of team play, but still from an unusual perspective. Those who coach or watch regularly will see that, up to the age of around 11 or 12, players will pass disproportionately to their best friends on the team, or to those players they perceive as being the best. They do so even when other team mates might be better placed.

This behaviour can be challenged, certainly from around the age of 8 or 9, but the coach should understand that it is a developmental factor that is causing this, not a lack of soccer awareness.

A great way of helping youngsters to develop the bigger picture is to make use of video clips and highlights of games. These are handy because they can be paused to illustrate a point. Highlights are useful because they also show poor decision making as well as great individual skills (which tend to be the focus of clips). It is also good for young players to see that even professionals at the top level of the game make mistakes, and that this is a valuable learning process.

Not every coach has access to a clubhouse with a TV or monitor, but laptops can be used and also parents can be asked to show their children at home, perhaps with a list of the sort of open ended questions which get the children thinking.

Unless we are coaching an older youth team, or an especially talented one, it is best not to label these sessions as 'tactics', which many kids see as boring. Rather, keep the sessions short, five minutes at most, and sell them on the basis of showing a goal, or picking some highlights from a big match.

The skilled coach then pauses the recording at various points and highlights the decisions made by players as they receive the ball. 'Why?' questions get children thinking. 'Why did Messi wait for that pass?' 'Why did Ozil not pass first time?' and so forth.

Control Drill – Big Picture

For this drill, we play a normal, or small sided, game. The coach tells the players that when the whistle is blown everybody must stand still immediately. He then asks players about their decisions, where they will run, how the receiver will accept the ball, where the defense will cover.

This sort of drill is effective if played regularly, for around ten minutes with the coach stopping the game about once per minute during that time. Any more, and the players become frustrated, less and the opportunity for making points about positioning and decision making is lost.

Receiving the Ball

Now that the player has made the decision about where they will receive the ball, and what they will do with it, next they must practice the skills of first touch, or control. It is important that, although first touch is the key skill in this aspect of the game, how they move, and what their decision will be informs *how* they receive the ball.

It is those vital fractions of a second which mean that the pass is delivered more quickly, and under less pressure and in the right way that marks out the very good player from the merely talented. We can use the analogy of catching a ball. The actual act of catching is relatively easy, as is passing or dribbling. However, it is about getting in the right place with the right body position that makes the catch straightforward. The same is true with soccer.

Controlling with the Foot

Inside of the foot

The safest and most common way of controlling the ball is with the inside of the foot. This is the basic control skill which should be taught first. The ball will strike the inside of the foot, and the touch should (unless there is significant pressure that will result in a tackle) move the ball around eight to twelve inches in front of the player after contact. This movement will be on a slight diagonal backwards if the receiver wishes for time on the ball before deciding on what should be done next, as the player can then get their body between the ball and an opponent, giving them time to make a decision.

There are a number of key techniques which young players need to acquire.

- Unless they have made a specific decision to wait for the ball, they move towards it.
- The ensure that their chest is in line with the arrival of the ball.
- The head moves forward slightly, which ensures their weight is over the ball. This will stop it from bouncing up and control being lost.

- Elbows and arms should be out to ensure best balance. This is very important for young children, for whom natural balance is still being acquired.
- The planted foot (the other to the one trapping the ball) should point to the direction of the ball, and be slightly wide of it.
- The trapping foot sits at right angles to the planted foot.
- The knee on the trapping leg is slightly bent forwards to ensure weight is over the ball once more.
- As the ball strikes the trapping foot, it drops back slightly to cushion the ball. The more it drops back the close to the body the ball will stop. However, if it drops too far, the ball will become stuck under the player's body, and they will need to dig it out in order to the play the ball. The good first touch leaves the ball ending a slight way away from the body, with the body protecting it from any opponent.

Control Drill – Basic Control; Inside of the Foot

This basic skill is one to be repeated even with older, and more skilled, players. It is the core element to keeping possession and an essential skill in a player.

The particular drill we are highlighting here is for more advanced players. It involves 6 v 2 working in a penalty area, or 20 x 10 m grid. The centre circle on a full sized pitch works as well.

The two players wear bibs to allow rapid change of role. It is a two touch possession game. Players receive the ball, remembering to glance to check the positioning of opponents. They must control the ball using the inside of the foot, and lay the ball off with their second touch.

If the opponent gets control of the ball, or it leaves the marked area, then the two defense players swap with the last two attackers to have touched the ball.

The drill can start simply with a 4 v 1 exercise; or three touches can be allowed instead of two. However, in match play situations, players will want to shift the ball quickly, hence the limited number of touches allowed on the ball.

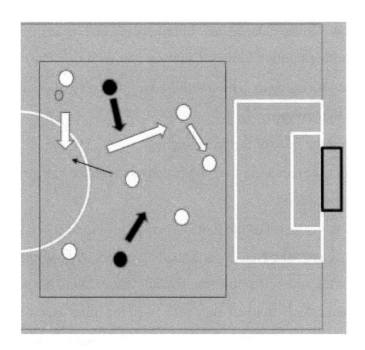

Outside of the foot

This is a much harder skill to acquire, and is used to enhance a player who is looking to turn quickly, either to gain a little space from a tight marker, or to continue to move the ball quickly in the direction it is travelling.

The key skills to practise are as follows:

- Move towards the ball.
- The shoulder on the receiving side is pointed towards the direction in which the ball is coming from.

- Arms out for balance, and to protect the ball (if an opponent is marking tightly).
- Lean forwards to get the weight over the ball and ensure it stays on the ground.
- Bend the knee of the receiving leg.
- Point the receiving foot slightly inwards so the ball strikes it on the outside.
- As the ball strikes the foot swivel the hips to turn quickly and move onto the ball. Note, usually a player will complete the quarter turn in the direction the ball is travelling, but sometimes, when closely marked, they may twist the other way to go round an opponent and trick them as to the direction the ball will travel.

Control Drill – Turning Using the Outside of the Foot

Use the key skills mentioned in the list of techniques given above. This drill uses semi opposition. The aim is for the striker to turn the defender, take a touch and shoot.

The drill involves two strikers – one to pass, one to shoot, and a defender. There is also a goalkeeper. Players rotate roles.

The defender should start by providing just limited opposition to all the strikers to practise their skills. Clearly, in a match situation, the defense would not know for sure that their striker was looking to turn and would adapt their defending accordingly.

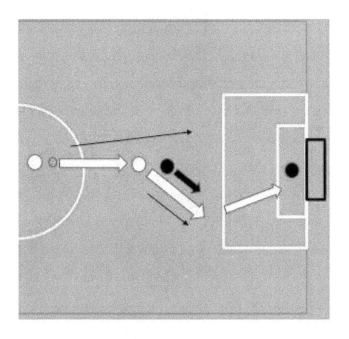

Controlling with the Thigh

We want young players to develop an approach to playing the game that keeps the ball on the deck. This makes it far easier to control, and therefore the next stage of a move easier to complete. Players are more effective when the game of soccer is played simply.

However, there will be times, for example from a long pass, a header or a throw in, when the ball needs to be controlled before it hits the floor.

The key skills to thigh control are below, and can be taught to kids through the drill that follows, Drill Six.

- Keep the knee low – it is a temptation for children, especially young ones who might lack co-ordination, to lift their thigh high. That is the part of the body they are going to use, and once their mind focusses on that, the thigh becomes the only part of their positioning they consider. If the knee goes too high (it should be angled below the horizontal) then the ball will bounce up, slowing down the speed of control and giving an opponent the opportunity to intercept. Also, balance is harder to maintain. Simply, the child might fall over. Amusing in a practice, frustrating in a match. (But still, as long as they are OK and find it so themselves, funny!)
- The eyes should watch the ball closely.
- The knee is directed so that the ball hits the thigh in the middle. That way it drops to the feet, and the sooner this occurs, the sooner it is possible to progress the move.
- When under pressure, and especially from throw ins, the player should look to side foot volley the dropping ball when it comes down from the thigh. The pass should be directed back the way it came. For example, back to the player who did the original throw.

Control Drill – Thigh Control

A simple drill that practises just what it sets out to improve. A whole squad of players can work on this drill at the same time. Divide the group into pairs. One of the pair (the feeder) uses the touchlines as their marker. The partner (the receiver) stands 10 metres back, using a cone to guide their starting point.

The feeder goes to their knees and lobs the ball to their partner. The receiver advances a couple of metres, controls the ball on their thigh using the technique outlined above, and lays the ball back to the feeder with a pass. The receiver then jogs back to their cone and advances ready to receive the ball on their other thigh. So the drill continues. Work for a minute on each player before swapping roles.

Controlling with the Chest

As we move further up the body so control becomes more difficult. Usually, with chest control the aim is to get the ball down to feet as quickly as possible and lay it off quickly. It is an essential skill for target man type strikers and defensive players who look to intercept and move the ball forward.

Key Skills

- Watch the ball all the way with the head in line with the ball. This automatically brings the feet into position.

31

- Arms wide for balance, and to make the chest area as large as possible.
- Angle the chest slightly upwards.
- Keep the arms out until the ball has dropped, as players are often under pressure when chesting the ball.
- Bring the ball down to feet quickly, in order to continue the move.

Control Drill – Chest Control

A good drill for chest control is to simply take drill six, and have the feeder throw the ball from a standing position. However, the drill below takes chest control a little further.

The ball is thrown in by player one. Player two controls with their chest and lays the ball off either to the person who made the throw in, or to a team mate. Moderate opposition is provided.

Top Tip: Tell players throwing underarm to aim for the head, the ball will then drop neatly at chest height.

The ball is passed across the width of the pitch under control, and the process starts again from the other side. There are five offensive and two defensive players involved in the drill.

To add an element of competition, the team tries to complete ten moves without losing control of the ball, or conceding possession. Coaches should begin with aiming for good technique and movement from their players, then add speed to the challenge, perhaps adding a time element to put add pressure onto the attacking side.

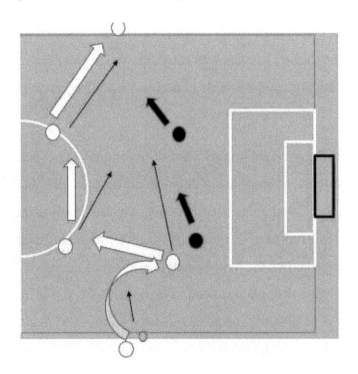

Controlling with the Head

There is much proper debate at the moment about heading footballs. The former England striker and Premier League leading ever scorer Alan Shearer recently took part in a television documentary examining the impact of heading the ball on the brain. The results were frightening, even for a fully grown adult. The concussive element of even gentle repeated headers was considerable. Shearer felt moderately tired quite quickly, and was able to perform simple cognitive tasks less quickly and with reduced accuracy.

Although the immediate impact wore off over time, the conclusion was that tiny amounts of damage are done whenever the ball is headed. Therefore, the global game is considering whether heading the ball should be removed from the youth game altogether. However, until a decision comes down this way or not, it is a part of the game. Therefore, it is a skill players need to learn. However, it is important to note that *it is beneficial to team play as well as players' health to keep the ball on the ground, which removes the potential for heading the ball.*

There are four purposes to heading the ball:

To gain height and distance with a defensive header;

To pass the ball to a team mate;

To use the header as a direct attempt on goal;

To control a high ball.

The technique for each is highly important (for safety reasons – heading the ball correctly does not eliminate concussive consequences, but appears to substantially reduce them) but does vary. We are looking here at the last example, heading to control the ball.

Note, this should be a last resort; if the ball can be allowed to run then that should be the option a player takes. However this will sometimes result in possession being lost.

In each of the following two ways of controlling with the head the arms should be out for balance, the head and neck muscles held firmly, eyes kept on the ball and open for as long as possible and the ball struck with the middle of the forehead (never the top of the head in this case).

Heading to Run On To a Ball: When a high ball is delivered to a player advancing with considerable space in front of them, they may choose to nod the ball forward to run on to. Here, the head leans forward and is angles slightly downwards to head the ball forwards and downwards. The player runs on to where they have nodded the ball.

Heading for Control: Here, the aim is to take the pace off the ball, rather like with chest control. It is a difficult skill, and if at all possible the player should aim to nod the ball to a team mate. However, that is not always possible. The ball is received chest on. The player angles their head slightly backwards at impact, and drops it slightly backwards to cushion the ball. The ball then bounces up slightly and down to feet, where it is controlled.

The player keeps their arms out all the time to give them greater balance and to protect the ball. It is often the case that the control goes from head to chest or thigh before hitting the ground, each manoeuvre taking more pace off the ball and making foot control easier.

Control Drill – Heading

If the decision is to undertake heading skills with children – the argument can be made that it is safer to learn the technique than head the ball incorrectly under the pressure of a match – then drills should be short, no more than five headers per drill, and only one drill per session.

Work in twos; one is feeder, one heads the ball. Decide which control will be used. If it is to run on to then the ball is thrown slightly in front of the player, if for personal control then straight to them.

Get the feeder to kneel, and lob the ball gently. With younger children, aged 10-11, dry sponge balls should be used, or even balloons, until the technique is acquired.

NOTE: *At the time of writing, in the US heading in soccer is banned for Under 10s, and allowed only in practices for those aged 11-13.*

Second Touch

We will not dwell for too long on this, other than to say that the better a player's first touch is, the easier the second touch becomes. Second touch is about decision making, whether to pass or dribble, protect or attack. As players progress they become quicker at making these decisions, until they have made them *before* the ball reaches them for their first touch.

This leads us neatly to the second stage of developing skills with youngsters. Once they have the ball under control, the best option is usually to pass – in the next chapter we will look at ways they can learn to do this.

Passing Skills

Get onto You Tube and have a search for clips of the great passers of the game. Players such as Xavi, the Spanish pocket battleship with the touch of the pianist; Andrea Pirlo who could control a game from deep, dictating play and creating chances.

Even better, show these great players in action to your own kids, or the ones in your team. Of course, the thundering tackle sets the heart racing with primeval passion; the curling shot brings a crowd to its feet; the amazing dribble tickles the emotions with an ever increasing touch. Those are the spectaculars of the game. But if that was all human beings cared about there would never be great novels; films would only be of the high action Marvel Comic style; poetry would not exist and nor would great drama. Art galleries would close rather than generate queues to see the masterpieces within. Michelangelo would have built houses instead of emotionally moving sculptures.

OK, perhaps we are going a little over the top here. But the point we are seeking to make is important. Passing is the cultural aspect of the game; the cerebral element which, at the highest level, supersedes all others. But kids like action, they like thunder and glory. Getting them to understand that passing is the heartbeat of soccer can prove to be a challenge.

Consider a group of seven year olds playing the game. The ball is rarely visible, lost beneath the morass of bodies chasing it. Occasionally, the child with a perspective on the state of play will find space and call for the pass. The chances of a team mate having the vision to spot that pass is low. Instead, the remaining players of each side are chasing hard...but without much thought.

So teaching the skill of passing when working with kids is a challenge. Nevertheless, the skilled and patient coach will achieve success. The first element of getting kids to pass is to constantly reinforce its value. But not in a way that criticises the basic instinct of kids to run with the ball. The coach stops play to highlight the pass; he or she showers praise on the player who finds space. The coach goes overboard with praise for the child who attempts a pass, whether successful or not.

Games are played whereby dribbling is banned. And only over time do young groups of players begin to utilise the power of the pass.

That is the point that focus can develop on improving the skills involved in the various kinds of pass that enhance the game.

Games to Instil a Culture of Passing

Young children love the game element of a training session. Actually so do older children, teens, adults and professionals. Admittedly, as the soccer ladder is climbed, so players develop a greater understanding of the importance of skill development, team play and both physical fitness and endurance. But let us be honest, it is the game that is the highlight of the session.

After all, if we did not enjoy competition, we would not play sport. Given this, it is a good idea to use games to develop the skills we want to see improved.

Passing Drill: Passing Game 3 v 3 with Mini Goals

This is a great starting point for a game. It can be played with three a side, or can go up to seven a side. Rondo style drills using the same principles can come in later. Here, one side will be weighted with players, and this team then have to devise ways to create opportunities and chances.

However, our basic drill operates on a 10 x 20 metre grid. Goals sit five metres in from either end. The goals are simply cones one metre apart. 'Goals' can be scored from in front or behind the goal. Tactically orientated players might work out that sticking a player between the posts stops any hope of scoring, which rather defeats the object of a drill which aims to develop passing.

Therefore it may be necessary to put into place some rules, such as an exclusion zone around the goals; another technique is to award one point for a shot and three for a goal. So although goals might not go in, the game because effectively 2 v 3, and the 3 players will win because it is easier for them to retain possession.

The game is simple. Allow four touches to begin, then reduce this gradually down to one touch as players get older and improve. Do not permit tackling or dribbling. Therefore, even with the four touch game, once a player has the ball under control they must pass. Focus on what the drill seeks to achieve – passing as a first choice – rather than the finer points of the rules of the game. With young children, they will find it hard to get out of their dribbling mind set, and inevitably more touches than are allowed will creep in.

Top Tip: *when working with children, keeping the objective of the drill at the forefront of thinking is key. Youngsters will make mistakes with the structure of a drill, that does not really matter as long as the key skill is being practised.*

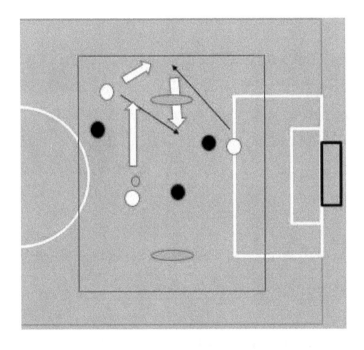

Short Passing

The very best teams use short passing to huge effect. Consider the decade of dominance of the Spanish national team and their club sides, especially Barcelona. Their success was built on a short passing game, known as tiki taka.

The advantages of short passing are that it is easier to be accurate, and since the ball will inevitably be on the floor, control for the receiving player is also more straightforward. However, speed is needed, and that means that first touch must be exact. The ball must be passed firmly, and no more than two touches should be used until the ball is passed on again.

The very best players develop the technique to using one touch passing to generate pace and movement.

The key skills of short passing are as follows:

- Use the instep.
- Strike firmly through the ball.
- Keep the head over the ball, to ensure it stays low.

44

- The non-kicking foot is planted firmly, and the arms are out for balance.
- Once the pass is complete, players move quickly to take up a position for a return pass.

Passing Drill: Short Passing Without Pressure

This is an excellent drill, pacy and involving all players.

The drill involves five players and takes place around a 10m square grid. A player occupies each side, and the fifth player holds the middle ground. A maximum of two touches are allowed, and one touch passing should be encouraged.

The ball is played into the central player, who controls and passes to a different player. That player passes back into the central player and so on. Every time a player passes they must move – the outside players along their line and the central player to a position so that they can receive the pass and turn quickly to play the next ball.

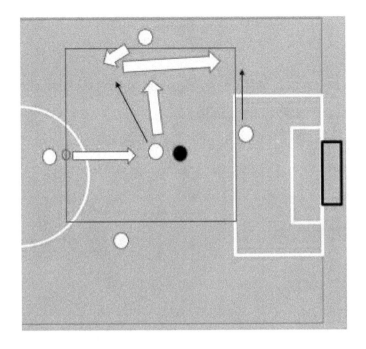

The drill can be developed easily. An opponent can be added to offer semi opposition to the central player. The central player does not have to receive every pass. The coach encourages touch, technique in passing, speed, movement and communication.

The last of these is very important. With short passing players must be on the same wavelength; that develops with verbal and physical communication. For example, call for the ball, indicating with the hands to where a pass needs to be played.

Passing Drill: Short Passing Rondo

In building their short passing game, the Barcelona coach Pep Guardiola developed the rondo – that is a drill with uneven sides. The great benefit of the rondo is that it provides some opposition, and therefore pressure. That makes the drill much closer to real life. However, the opposition is limited, and the dominant side should get plenty of opportunity to practise the skill in question.

So some game type situation being used, but not the kind of match play where the skill in question is lost within the dynamics that are created when sides are evenly matched in a competitive situation.

The rondo below can be adapted to the needs and skills of a team. Certainly, talented Under 8s and above can use this kind of drill.

The objective is to maintain possession. A small grid is used; the size of the grid depends to an extent on the age and ability of the players. For example, a good Under 12 side might use a 10 x 5 metre grid, whereas Under 9s might use a 10 x 10 m grid.

The drill involves six players. Use two coloured bibs to identify the opposition. This allows quick change around of roles, keep the drill moving and the players interest maintained. There are no goals, and the objective is to keep possession. Through one or two touch short passing, good communication and movement possession is retained. Each time it is lost, or the ball leaves the grid, the last person to play it swaps roles with one of the defenders, and the game continues.

Top Tip: when working with children, keeping the objective of the drill at the forefront of thinking is key. Youngsters will make mistakes with the structure of a drill, that does not really matter as long as the key skill is being practised.

Mid-Range Passing – Inside and Outside of the Foot

Inside of the Foot

Some young players seem to be blessed with passing ability. Not only do they 'see' the pass, but they have the innate technique to deliver the ball as well. However, for most passing skills need to be worked on.

Coaches should focus on technique. The following are key elements towards delivering a mid-range pass – one of more than 10 to 15 metres.

- Head up: if players have their heads down, they cannot see the pass they wish to make.
- Body position: For the pass arms should be out for balance and the non-kicking foot firmly planted. Head is over the ball and facing the direction of the pass.
- Strike the ball firmly with the instep, and follow through smoothly.
- The ball will curve slightly inwards as it loses pace, and there should be an allowance for this in the direction of the pass.

Top Tip: Right from the youngest age encourage players to get their heads up and looking around. One of the (many) reasons that young players are reluctant to pass is that they concentrate their eyes on the ball, rather than the game around them. As the ball is delivered to them, they should be assessing their next move.

Outside of the Foot

This is a great pass for getting the ball from a central position to a wide attacking part of the pitch. It is a riskier pass than the inside of the foot delivery, but should be a part of every player's armoury.

An outside of the foot pass applies more swerve and so is great for putting the ball into space behind a narrow defense.

- The process is the same as for the instep pass, until it comes to striking the ball.
- The ball is struck with the outside of the foot, with contact from just behind the little toe. This imparts spin, the effect of which comes into play as the ball slows.
- The kicking foot continues in a straight line, while the ball heads off at an angle. The pass should be aimed straight if it is to swerve outwards for an on-running player.
- Generally, a pass with the outside of the food needs to be struck with more force than one struck with the inside. This is because there is less direct contact between foot and ball.

A good warm up is to get two or three players standing around 10 - 20 metres apart, depending on the age of the children. They practise striking the ball with the inside and outside of the foot, so that they learn about pace and direction, and also practice controlling the ball. Keep this kind of warm up relaxed but active. Encourage players to pass with their weaker foot as well as their stronger one. A two footed player is far more effective and versatile than one who overly relies on one foot or the other.

Passing Drill: The Pass in Behind – Inside and Outside of the Foot

This is a fairly complex drill. However, it is good for many reasons. It provides opportunities for passing with the inside and the outside of the foot. It is fast paced. It ends with a shot, and so is one that children enjoy.

The drill involves two players and a keeper, but works best with a second keeper and between 8 and 12 players. These line up as passers and wingers, and work in pairs. The keepers swap after each drill, returning the soccer ball so the waiting pair always have a ball ready to use.

Half a seven a side pitch is ideal. Four cones spread across the width of the area, and around 5 metres in front of it represent a defensive line. Player one dribbles from the half way line to the edge of the centre circle. The coach gets him or her to focus on keeping their head up. They pass between central defender cone and full back cone. Passes should be with both the inside and the outside of the foot. Player two has sprinted on outside the full back cone and running onto the pass. Player one continues their run to the edge of the box. Player two delivers a pass with the inside of the foot, and player one runs on to shoot first time, or after a touch.

The players head back to the starting positions ready to go again, but this time player two will start with the ball, and player one makes the run down the wing.

After a while attack the opposite wing so players get used to using both feet.

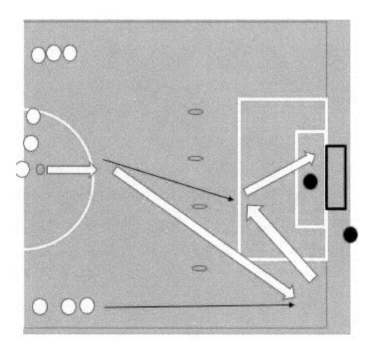

Long, Lifted Pass

Soccer is a sport best played on the ground. The object is to score a goal; that doesn't happen without possession of the ball, and the ball is best held on to when it is on the ground. Once the ball leaves the ground accuracy is compromised, the pass must, by definition, be long and that makes accuracy more difficult to achieve. If the pass is accurate, controlling it is more of a challenge than if the ball has been received along the ground.

However, there is a place for the long pass. It offers variety and can move the ball quickly over long distances. Excluding crosses, which are a specific offensive tool, there are two main uses of the long ball.

Firstly is the ball down the wing. Often played by full backs, the ball is either played to be controlled on the chest of the striker, or hit into the space behind the opposing full back for a winger to run on to. This allows very quick transition of play, and it is during transition that spaces most often open up.

The other pass is the cross field one which aims to switch play, dragging a defense across the pitch and creating spaces for strikers to exploit. Usually this kind of pass is played directly to the wide player.

A little note. Sometimes centre halves look to lump the ball forward. But this is a pass of limited value. Because the delivery is straight and central there is a tiny margin for error. Defenders can easily intercept or, if the pass lacks precision, the ball simply runs through to the keeper and possession is lost.

Technique for the long pass is as follows.

- Set the ball at 45 degrees to the body.
- Arms out for balance.
- Strike the ball with the toes, low down so the foot goes slightly under the ball.
- Lean slightly back, keeping the head still.
- Strike through the ball and continue the arc of the foot.
- Re balance by bring the alternate arm across the kicking foot in a scissor shape.
- The ball will curl with the direction of the foot.

Passing Drill – Long Pass Game

Although this drill is complicated, and children might need a few tries to get the idea, once it is understood it is great for developing accuracy with the long pass. It also promotes communication, team play and shooting skills. Oh, and it is good fun. It works well with good Under 10s and above.

The drill involves half a seven a side pitch, with a goal at each end. The pitch is divided into three zones. At either end the zone is half the size as the central zone (approximately 10 metres, 20 metres and 10 metres. Lots of balls are needed.

The drill is six a side, one goalkeeper, one defender, one forward and three midfielders.

Defenders: Play the long pass, missing out the midfield. Defend their area of the pitch.

Strikers: Attempt to score or set up a team mate.

Midfielders: The most complex position. They must work together to provide support under restricted conditions. When the ball is possession in their defensive zone ONE midfielder goes into this area to support the defender and keeper. They may play the long ball to the attacking zone.

When the ball is played into the attacking zone ONE midfielder may join it to support their striker. The midfielder can score goals, or set up the attacker. If the ball goes to the keeper, or the defender wins possession, the midfielder must withdraw from the attacking zone.

If the ball enters the midfield zone, the players may pass to either zone, or shoot.

When the ball is under the possession of their opponents in either the attacking or defensive zone they MUST NOT enter the zone, and if they are in it, they MUST LEAVE it immediately. Thus, communication is needed to work out the best placed midfielder to do the relevant job.

The game is played. Each time the ball goes out of play a new one is returned by the coach to the relevant team in the relevant zone. Thus, a shot going wide results in the new ball given to the keeper for the restart. A corner results in the ball given to the striker/midfielder in the attacking zone. Players should swap positions regularly.

Be patient with the drill. It does take children a while to get the idea, but once they do it is a drill that can be used regularly to develop long ball passing.

Top Tip: With drills like this, young players will often seek to pre plan. For example, the dominant midfielder will make it clear that he is the one who will support the attack! Do not allow this. The players must learn to react to the situation facing them, with movements made by the players in the best positions.

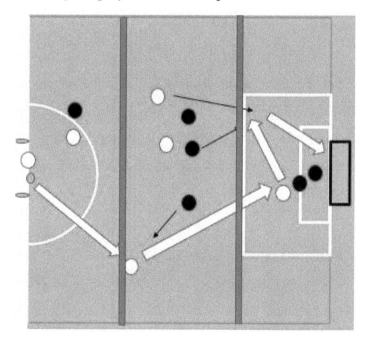

Using Cones to Improve Passing

A key element of coaching young players is to keep them busy. A good warm up is to set up a 'passing assault course'. These are cones to encourage passing accuracy. Short, long and mid-range passes can be practised, using the cones to create angles. Get the players to work in twos or threes, and have them moving around the course every minute or so.

If staffing allows, a course can be set up by one coach while another works on a different skill. As any of us who have worked with youth teams, keeping pace in the session is vital for maintaining interest and enjoyment for younger players.

Offensive Skills

Had George Best been from a major footballing nation he would be mentioned in the same breath as Pele, Maradona, Messi. Perhaps he actually is. He shared many of their talents; superb dribbling skills; smallish stature (although at 5' 9" he just about made average height even though his slender frame made him appear much smaller.) The other vital attribute Best shared with those greats was a deadly eye for goal.

The Northern Irishman once scored no less than six times in a single match. It was against Northampton Town in the FA Cup tournament and the remarkable event occurred back in 1970. Certainly, there was a gulf in class and league position between the teams, but it was still a remarkable performance. The astonishing display was even more noteworthy when it is considered that the game took place in conditions where the grass had more in common with a farmyard than a soccer pitch. The fans of both sides who were sitting and standing in Northampton's infamous two and half sided ground were given a memorable treat. That was on top of the unique experience of watching a top level match in the only professional stadium missing one and a half of its stands in Britain and possibly the world (literally, there was nothing there).

(It's a little known fact outside of the shoe making town that Northampton Town's relatively new stadium also lacks a side. It's not cricket or bowls this time that takes out an end, as it was in the 1970s, but some financial impropriety. One side of Northampton's Sixfields Stadium was given permission to be graced by a new, two tier stand only for it to be left to stand gaping like a toothless baby as the money ran out before the structure could be completed! Now that is useful soccer related trivia for a post-match chat in the bar!)

But back to Best. Sadly everything went wrong for him when his superstar status imploded in a fugue of women and alcohol. But Best's fame was guaranteed. Most readers will have heard of the tricky striker, many will know of his exploits well. So here's another question. Brazil won the World Cup in 1970. Who made up their defense? Tricky, eh? Because, even though some consider Brazil team of 1970 to be the greatest ever international side we know the striker of Northern Ireland, but not the defense of this amazing group of World Cup winners.

Useful Note: In fact, it was Carlos Alberta, captain and right back, Piazza and Brito in the centre and at left back was Everaldo.

So it isn't surprising that kids all want to be a striker; a center forward, number 10 or winger. Maybe there will be the odd seven year old who sees themselves as a midfielder, or defensive player, but they are few and far between.

Still, in the modern game everybody can be an offensive player. The old notion of schoolboy soccer that the full backs do not cross the half way line is thankfully dead and buried. No longer are the only requirements of a center to be big and have the ability to kick the ball half the length of the pitch. Nowadays, offense begins with the goalie, and develops from there.

Finding Space

Lessons learned when we are young stay with us for life. Finding space at kids' level is not so hard. Provided, of course, that the youngsters have learned to pass the ball. Small sided games are designed so that players have time and space when they are in possession. After all, skills are not going to develop if players are closed down as soon as the ball arrives at their feet.

That does not mean that the skills of finding space need not be taught. We might divide this aspect of soccer into five stages.

Number One – Recognizing Space: This is all about getting players to have their heads up. Youngsters tend to focus on the ball, but we need to encourage them to see the big picture (a point to which we return time after time when we are coaching kids). There is an ancient Chinese proverb which we can apply to teaching the skill of recognizing space – in fact, the proverb provides a good maxim for learning of any kind. It goes like this:

I hear…and I forget

I see…and I remember

I do…and I understand.

In other words, just telling our young players to find space, or to move to a particular place, has little worth. They might do it, and it could give some immediate benefit. But five minutes later the coach will be saying the same thing. Setting players out so that they can see spaces is better, players will have an idea of where to go, but not why. Therefore they will find it hard to react to new situations. But getting them to discover their own space is best of all.

We can do this through repetition. Remember, kids need to be active. They learn when they are 'doing' (haven't we seen that idea somewhere before?!). So these skills are best acquired through the game situation. It can be the end of session 'match' that kids so adore. It can be a specifically set up rondo session with a focus on finding space. The coach needs to be active in setting questions to the children. 'What should our eyes be doing?' 'What do we do with our heads?' 'Where do we move?' 'Why have you moved there?' These questions are backed up with lots of praise. Soon, our young charges will be finding space by second nature. When they move on to full 11 a side soccer, that skill will stand them in good stead.

Two Stage Runs: We will look at making runs more specifically later on in the chapter. However, a good defense and midfield will limit space. Players can create it by making runs in two stages. Firstly, they fix in their head where they want the space to be, then drift away from that area. This takes a defender with them, creating the space in the zone they want. Next, they sprint back into the space they have created. This move is sometimes called a zig-zag.

Timing: How many times do we hear the TV commentator state: 'He timed his run to perfection'? But achieving such a high level of perfection takes practice. And teamwork. Players need to play together so that they begin to understand when a pass is likely to be delivered, and when a team mate likes to make their run. The great Dutch master Dennis Bergkamp was a genius at this. Look up on You Tube some clips of his assists. Yes, he could play the 40 yard inch perfect Crossfield ball, but his real skill was the ten yard pass, delivered with perfect weight, to match the sprint of his strike partner.

Small sided games are best for developing timing, since players get plenty of touches on the ball.

Where to Run – Turning the Defense: Defenders like to be able to see both the ball and the threat of their opponent. Therefore, if a striker plays 'on the shoulder' of his marker, in other words, with the defender between her and the ball, then that defender has to try to look in two places at the same time. The striker then has a half second advantage when making their run. We will look at this in a little more detail later in the chapter.

Fluidity: A crucial aspect of the game, this. And also one that is very hard for youngsters to learn. As adults, we know that scoring a goal is usually the work of great team play. That the person who scores has done well, but space for that player has been created by others who do not receive the same levels of glory. Kids find that concept hard to understand. By constantly praising movement that creates space for others, young sides will develop better coordination in their team play, and become a proper unit rather than a group of individuals.

We would not advocate specific drills for finding space. Creating such a scenario is extremely artificial. Instead, we suggest that this is a skill constantly reinforced through other drills and, especially, match situations – conditioned or real. Coaches should be prepared to blow their whistle and bring proceedings to a halt. This gives them the chance to point out good play. They should also be prepared to speak to individuals while the game is continuing to point out ways in which they could find space more effectively.

We know from our understanding of child development that spatial awareness is a condition that develops over time. We cannot change that, but what we can do is maximize the potential a child has to recognize space on the pitch. That way, by the time they reach the age where they can see the big picture of a soccer match, they will have the skills and knowledge to create and utilize space.

Offside

It's a nightmare. That super striker who could not stop scoring at Under 11 level, suddenly can't get a touch at Under 12s. Worse, every time your side attacks, he runs offside and possession is lost. It's a frighteningly common scenario. And totally not the fault of the young forward, but of a lack of club structure across the age groups.

This fault is often created by a 'win at all costs' mentality which places short term gain above long term development, and comes back to bite when the structure of the game changes.

For this reason, we advocate playing as though offside were a rule from a much younger age than Under 12. Perhaps start even as young as Under 10. It might cost the team the odd goal in matches. However, it will make the transition at the point offside becomes a law much easier to achieve. (In any case leaving a striker upfield unmarked – 'goal hanging' as we used to call it – is not a great tactic under most circumstances. The 'goal hanger' becomes peripheral to the match which leaves the team short in midfield. Leaving a striker up and alone also promotes playing the long ball, since the team will be seeking to get the ball forward before the defense can re-organize.).

The Law of Offside Explained: Apologies if this seems like a little waste of space, but we feel it is worth pointing out the tenets of offside.

Law 11 is the most complex in soccer. Just watch pundits argue about whether so and so was offside when the ball was put into the net, whether they were interfering with play as their team mate scores. If your main job is as a referee or linesman (sorry, assistant referee!) please skip this brief section. But it is handy to remind ourselves of the intricacies of the law. If we do not fully grasp it ourselves, how can we teach it to our young team?

Here we quote from the Football Association website, www.thefa.com. Observations and illustrations are in non-italic font.

Offside position

It is not an offence to be in an offside position. (Teams frequently set up these days with players standing in offside positions. This causes issues for the defense as they decide whether to drop back to mark the player, causing there to be more space for other opponents, or leave the player and risk him being in a strong position a couple of passes down the line. Despite the risk, this last option is the most popular.)

A player is in an offside position if:

• *any part of the head, body or feet is in the opponents' half (excluding the halfway line) and*

any part of the head, body or feet is nearer to the opponents' goal line than both the ball and the second-last opponent

• *The hands and arms of all players, including the goalkeepers, are not considered.*

A player is not in an offside position if level with the:

- *second-last opponent or*
- *last two opponents*

(Note: while this will nearly always include the goalkeeper, it does not have to. So, just because a defender is closer to the line than the attacker does not exclude her from being offside if the keeper is further up the pitch.)

Offside offence

A player in an offside position at the moment the ball is played or touched* by a team-mate is only penalised on becoming involved in active play by:

interfering with play by playing or touching a ball passed or touched by a team-mate or

- *interfering with an opponent by:*

69

- *preventing an opponent from playing or being able to play the ball by clearly obstructing the opponent's line of vision or*
  - *challenging an opponent for the ball or*
- *clearly attempting to play a ball which is close when this action impacts on an opponent or*
  - *making an obvious action which clearly impacts on the ability of an opponent to play the ball*
  *The first point of contact of the 'play' or 'touch' of the ball should be used

or

  - *gaining an advantage by playing the ball or interfering with an opponent when it has:*
- *rebounded or been deflected off the goalpost, crossbar or an opponent* (Note the word 'deflected' here. Simply because the ball rebounds does not put a player onside.)
  - *been deliberately saved by any opponent*
- *A player in an offside position receiving the ball from an opponent who deliberately plays the ball (except from a deliberate save by any opponent) is not considered to have gained an advantage.*
(Note that the opponent playing the ball must do so deliberately, and not in the process of making a 'block' or save. This is often the cause of controversy since the referee must make a judgement as to whether

70

when a defender plays the ball he is attempting a clearance or pass – the striker is not offside – or the ball either deflects off of her by accident or in the process of making a save – offside.)

A 'save' is when a player stops, or attempts to stop, a ball which is going into or very close to the goal with any part of the body except the hands/arms (unless the goalkeeper within the penalty area).

In situations where:

a player moving from, or standing in, an offside position is in the way of an opponent and interferes with the movement of the opponent towards the ball this is an offside offence if it impacts on the ability of the opponent to play or challenge for the ball; if the player moves into the way of an opponent and impedes the opponent's progress (e.g. blocks the opponent) the offence should be penalised under Law 12

- *a player in an offside position is moving towards the ball with the intention of playing the ball and is fouled before playing or attempting to play the ball, or challenging an opponent for the ball, the foul is penalised as it has occurred before the offside offence*

- *an offence is committed against a player in an offside position who is already playing or attempting to play the ball, or challenging an opponent for the ball, the offside offence is penalised as it has occurred before the foul challenge*

71

No offence

There is no offside offence if a player receives the ball directly from:

- *a goal kick*
- *a throw-in*
- *a corner kick*

Offences and sanctions

If an offside offence occurs, the referee awards an indirect free kick where the offence occurred, including if it is in the player's own half of the field of play.

A defending player who leaves the field of play without the referee's permission shall be considered to be on the goal line or touchline for the purposes of offside until the next stoppage in play or until the defending team has played the ball towards the halfway line and it is outside their penalty area. If the player left the field of play deliberately, the player must be cautioned when the ball is next out of play. (A tricky one here, because if a player is injured and rolls just off the pitch on the goal line, they are playing the other side onside. However, from a sportsmanship point of view to score a goal in that situation pushes the bounds of fair play to the limit.)

An attacking player may step or stay off the field of play and not to be involved in active play. If the player re-enters from the goal line and becomes involved in play before the next stoppage in play, or the defending team has played the ball towards the halfway line and it is outside their penalty area, the player shall be considered to be positioned on the goal line for the purposes of offside. A player who deliberately leaves the field of play and re-enters without the referee's permission and is not penalised for offside and gains an advantage, must be cautioned.

If an attacking player remains stationary between the goalposts and inside the goal as the ball enters the goal, a goal must be awarded unless the player commits an offside offence or Law 12 offence in which case play is restarted with an indirect or direct free kick.

Useful Note: *Law 12 relates to fouls and misconduct. In other words, offences which incur free kicks – direct or indirect – and penalty kicks.*

The good news (probably) is, of course, that at schoolboy or girl level, such intricacies are rarely applied. That is one of the reasons why we would never advocate setting up a youth team to play an offside trap. Not only does it place tactics over skill development, which should never be the case, but it rarely works.

The secret to avoid falling offside lies in the timing of runs, ideas of which come at the end of this chapter. Timing of runs is a skill whether offside is in operation or not. That is another reason why playing as though the rule is in place is wise whichever age group we coach.

Wide Play

A soccer pitch is relatively wide. The most advantageous position to be in space is in the middle of the pitch, since most options are available from here. However, that is the most densely packed area. Good teams use width, because that is where the space both is, and is most easily created.

Transition is the change of possession from one team to another. Good sides try to stay narrow, restricting space, when out of possession, and send players wide when they win it back, exploiting space.

Offensive Drill: Creating Width

This is a handy drill because, although conditioned, it does recreate the transition stage of a game. The drill requires half a pitch. There are three defenders, a goalkeeper (who begins the drill in position) and five attackers. Therefore, this is a rondo drill where the attacking side should be successful in their aim of getting a shot on goal. The ball starts on the center spot. There are flags or cones marking the half way line and corner spots.

The defenders begin where the halfway line meets the touchline. The attackers by the opposite corner flag. The drill begins with players sprinting along the touch line, around a flag and into position. Therefore, like in transition, players have to work hard to get into the correct defensive or offensive positions. The offensive team use their two spare players to create width on both sides of the pitch. The side's aim is to get the ball wide and into space to allow a cross which gives them a goal scoring opportunity.

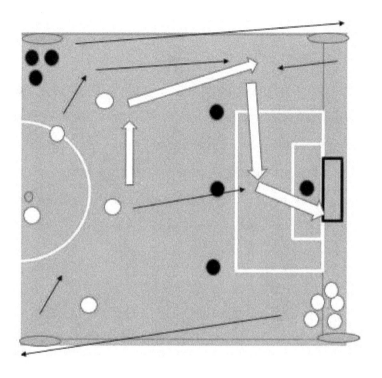

Note: For this drill we have duplicated the players, showing both their starting positions and the positions they can adopt when the ball comes into player. So, for example, the huddle of whites are the same players as the spread out group close to the half way lane.

Dribbling

An exciting offensive skill. Coaches should encourage players to use both feet. They should demonstrate and allow players to practice individual dribbling skills, such as the step over, or drop of the shoulder. When running with the ball (i.e., when there is space in front of the player) coaches look for players to move the ball with their laces, and knock it in front of them to allow fast movement without breaking stride.

Top Tip: Encourage these skills, always rewarding the effort even if it does not come off. Only be enjoying themselves will players experiment, and thus properly challenge themselves to improve.

Dribbling is a great warm up activity, and the following drill can be used and adapted every session since it is simple to use, involves every player (even a keeper needs good footwork in the modern game), is pacy and needs little direct coaching.

Offensive Drill: Dribbling warm up.

Half the length of the pitch. Players start at one end. A series of cones are placed close together for close dribbling skills. There is a space midway for players to try their individual skill. At the end, turn around the larger cone, run with the ball at speed until the final marker, when a pass is made to the next available player. Continue to the back of the line.

By placing a different colored cone at the appropriate point, the next player will know when to set off. Keep the drill moving, there can be at least four players working at any one time.

Shooting

The speed and accuracy with which a player can shoot will determine the success of a team. Therefore, shooting should be a skill practised regularly. Never discourage shooting, even if a shot is mis-hit. There is an old saying, and it is so true. 'You can't score if you don't shoot.' And players won't shoot if they are worried about the consequences of missing.

The key elements of a good shot are as follows:

- Set the ball at around 45 degrees to the body.
- Set the arms out for balance and plant the non-kicking foot securely beside the ball.

- Keep the head over the ball to keep the shot down.
- Strike with the laces, hitting through the ball.
- Follow through smoothly.
- Aim for the far corner of the goal. Aim to keep the shot low, which is harder for the keeper.

There are many shooting drills. We like the one below because it involves movement, and can be developed with the addition of a defender.

Offensive Drill: Pass and Shoot

A goalkeeper and three strikers are involved, with others waiting to join in. Two cones are positioned. in line with the corner of the penalty box, and about 5 meters back from it. Players two and three are placed on these posts.

Player one starts on the edge of the center circle. He passes firmly and along the ground to either other player, and runs on. The player who receives the ball either sets up a shot for the striker, or passes to his other teammate, who then sets up the shot.

The striker times his run for a first or second touch shot.

79

Players rotate to ensure all have time to work on the key skill being practiced here.

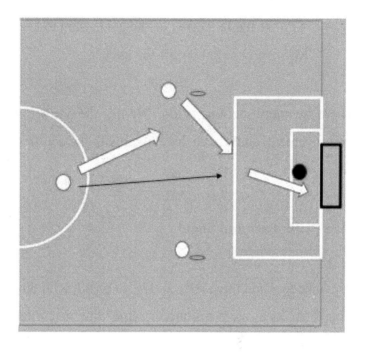

Timing Runs

Finally, we have arrived. Like a striker getting onto the end of a cross, or a midfielder arriving late into space, we have reached the frequently referred to major skill of this chapter. We have constantly emphasized the importance of timing runs. If we teach this attribute to young players, they will have it at their feet (literally speaking) for their entire playing lives.

A well timed run sees the player arrive in space at the same time as the ball. It involves a good understanding between team mates; they must know where and when the player will time his run, he or she must understand how his team mate will deliver their pass.

Playing together regularly helps, players keeping their heads up is even more important. Communication with words or gestures is key. However good the understanding between two players it is not, as hyperbolic commentators like to suggest, telepathic. It is the result of playing together, spotting spaces and communicating well.

Into the blind spot

The blind spot is the space behind a defender that is not captured in their peripheral vision. When strikers operate in the blind spot, they can gain a valuable second to find space or get a shot away.

Offensive Drill: Into the Blind Spot.

This is a rondo drill, with four against two plus a keeper. One player delivers the pass. In this version, there are two central players who are marked, plus the fourth player who stays wide. The strikers move towards the ball, leaving their defender goal side of them.

They twist and run in behind the defender, and the ball is passed inside the defender either to the wide player, or the striker who has made their run. The striker uses the space they have created to get a shot away. Other players support to provide options or pick up rebounds.

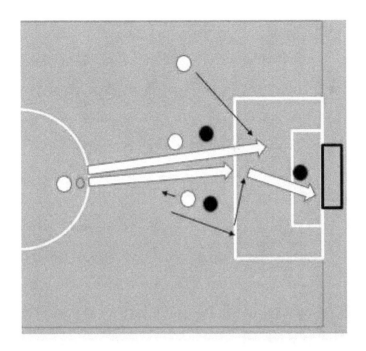

Bending a run to avoid offside

With all but the youngest kids playing the sport the concept of bending the run will be used more effectively if there is understanding behind it.

Certainly, it is an essential skill for a striker if offside is being played. Even when it is not, learning the skill early is no bad thing. Principally, the move achieves the following benefits:

- The striker is already moving and can therefore accelerate more effectively.
- The striker knows when he or she is going to bend their run, and that gives them an advantage over a defender.
- The defense is turned. Defenders prefer to defend with their backs to goal, not running towards their own danger area.
- Making a tackle from behind is far more difficult than a tackle from the side, or a block tackle. Even if the ball is won, there is a risk that the defender will come through the attacker to win the ball, giving away a free kick.
- A mis-timed tackle from behind can often result in a red card if it stops a striker who is away on goal. This does not usually apply in youth soccer.
- Turning a defense causes it to lose its shape, creating more space for other players.
- Finally, when the striker bends their run successfully and the through pass is accurate, a goal scoring opportunity is often created.

However, a good understanding is needed between striker and play maker. That relationship is developed in training and through playing together. Nevertheless, the successful striker learns when it is a good time and not so wise to try a bending run.

When the midfielder in possession is being heavily pressed, making a defense splitting pass is much harder to achieve. In these situations a good striker is better employed by making a short run towards the midfielder giving them an easier pass. When the midfielder has space, however, that is a good time to bend a run and head for the space in behind the defense.

The best strikers also develop an awareness of their team mates. It may be that making a short run towards the ball gives a fellow player a better opportunity of bending their run into the space which has just been created.

Finally, with young players, it is really important that making runs is rewarded with praise. The majority of the time the striker will bend their run, set off with a burst of acceleration only to have to pull up because the pass is not delivered. This can be demoralizing for the striker, who needs to understand the importance of making their moves. Being a number 9 is not all about scoring great goals and getting the glory…it is also about hard work.

A good message to give to young players is that the center forward is often the first person to be replaced tactically in the professional game. The usual reason for this is that the striker has made so many runs - many not resulting in them receiving a pass – that they need a break!

Offensive Drill: Bending the run.

The set up for this drill is the same as for Drill 17 A. However, in this example the strikers start from a slightly deeper position on the pitch, leaving more space for in behind the defense for passer to supply the ball. Offside applies.

Useful Note: Starting a little farther up the pitch might be dictated by the defense. Tactically, a higher line squeezes the midfield making a key pass harder to achieve, but the down side is that the defense leaves more space in behind it for a quick offensive player to exploit.

The three attacking players split one wide on each side, and one centrally. They run laterally across the pitch, and indicate when the pass is to be made. At that moment they change direction and sprint towards the goal, using their defender for purchase if they are marked.

Note, this needs to be legal shoulder to shoulder contact. The ball is played into the space behind the defense. This is probably the easiest way of timing a run since there is the biggest margin for error.

Breaking from Midfield

Offensive Drill – Breaking from Midfield

So onto the most complex way of breaching the offside trap. To create space for a break from midfield requires great team work. Here, each player has an individual task. Player one will pass the ball into space for the midfield runner.

Player two comes towards the ball, taking his defender with him. At the same time player three peels wide with a lateral run to take his defender wide. This player will then change the direction of his run towards goal to support the midfielder if required.

Player four, the midfield runner, angles his run into the space created by his team mates. The pass and run should be timed to allow the player to be as close to the offside line as possible, which gives them most opportunity to utilize their break to create a goal scoring opportunity.

Begin the drill by walking through the moves to get the players used to their role, then increase the tempo. The drill then moves onto its third stage by playing a 4 v 2 (plus a keeper) game where the offensive team need to create goal scoring opportunities. If the offensive team are struggling, an additional player can be added to their side to increase their passing options.

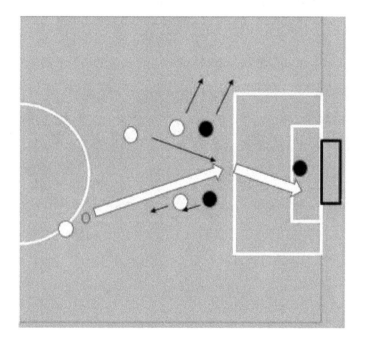

We have been fairly technical in this chapter on offensive play. Kids can cope with this type of technical training provided that it is fun, active and the coach encourages players to experiment and offers no criticism when they go wrong.

However, coaches also need to be aware of limiting young people's play. While all will benefit technically from the drills that have been presented in this chapter, we must also be aware of not restricting the creativity of young people. It is this creativity that will enable a very good young player to turn into an exceptional one.

The best coaches use their judgement and are not bound by the coaching manual.

A Short message from the Author:

Hey, are you enjoying the book? I'd love to hear your thoughts!

Many readers do not know how hard reviews are to come by, and how much they help an author.

I would be incredibly thankful if you could take just 60 seconds to write a brief review on Amazon, even if it's just a few sentences!

Browse to the product page and leave a review as shown below.

Thank you for taking the time to share your thoughts!

Your review will genuinely make a difference for me and help gain exposure for my work.

Defensive Skills

There is a sad irony about the beginning of this chapter. I had just sat down, research at the ready, to put pen to paper (or, at least, finger to keyboard) when my Twitter feed beeped. The message was a particularly sad one. Gordon Banks had died.

Banks was, of course, the keeper who made 'that save'. He also won the world cup with England - their only victory occurring back in 1966 when they were on home soil. He was voted by FIFA as the world's top goalkeeper no less than six times. Famously, his career was cut short when he lost an eye in a car crash in the early 1970s. Still, he went on to play again in the newly formed MLS at the end of that decade. Imagine that, a one eyed keeper playing at what was still a relatively high level.

But he made 'that save.' It is the 1970 World Cup in Mexico. Favourites Brazil are playing England, cup holders, in Guadalajara. It is a group stage match, but for most pundits it is the final come early. The Brazil side of 1970 is considered the greatest national team of all time. That is a view held by many whose opinion we should respect.

Carlos Alberta sends a perfectly weighted pass wide to Jairzinho. The great winger skips past Terry Cooper, the England full back, as though he were a training ground mannequin and floats a deep cross in towards the far post. Jairzinho was the second best player in the world at the time; his name would be even better known today had not the greatest player in the world – not only in 1970 but of all time – also been a member of his team.

In fact that player, the incomparable Pele, of course, is on the receiving end of the cross. He finds space on the far post and, unmarked and just seven yards out, rises with perfect timing. His header is textbook. Powerful, in the corner and downwards.

But that is not all. Such is the combination of power on the header and hardness in the ground that the ball bounces up viciously two yards from the goal line. So much so that as it reaches that line, it is half way up the goal.

Pele turns, raises his arm and shouts 'Goal!' (A story he tells with such good humour and unassuming modesty – a few modern day players and coaches could take a lesson there.) Now let us consider the developing play from the perspective of Gordon Banks. As Jairzinho passes Cooper he has a clear run on goal. Therefore Banks is drawn to protect his near post. The cross is firm. The header perfect. In order to stop the ball Banks must perform not just one but four pieces of magic.

Firstly, he must scurry across the entire width of the goal. Secondly he must fling himself, but in a controlled way that will allow him a microsecond to adjust for the bounce of the ball. Thirdly, he must change his arm position while still in the air. Remember, the header is powerful, the bounce high and unpredictable. The ball hits the ground just a yard and a half in front of him. Effectively, he has no time at all to make that adjustment. Finally, he must have the strength in his hands to push the ball wide. He does it all. If you haven't seen it, watch the save on line. Show it to your kids, your team – in fact anybody who is around. But make sure you are sitting down when you do.

But the save is more than just unbelievable. It sums up the message of this chapter (and, in many ways, this book). Gordon Banks was an incredibly modest man. Although the greatest goal keeper in the world, his time was before the enormous influx of money that influences the game today. Where he playing today, a man with his outrageous talent would demand a transfer fee of $120,000,000 at the very least, and a salary of $350,000 per week.

Not, though, in the 1960s and 70s. The world cup winners received under $1500 for their exploits in 1966. The unsustainable bubble of increasing fees and wages that must surely burst one day – covering everything soccer related under its sticky detritus -was many years in the future. But despite a relatively meagre financial return from his outstanding achievements in the game, Banks was always in demand for after dinner speeches. He would take some memento along to events, perhaps a shirt he had swapped, or some gloves he had worn, and at the end of his talk he would auction the item off to the highest bidder. Imagine, owning a pair of gloves worn by the greatest goalkeeper the world has ever seen. The money raised would not see the lining of his pocket, but would be passed on immediately to the children's ward of the local hospital.

Passed to the hospital quietly. Without fuss or fanfare. In fact, the story only came out as friends reminisced about the great man on the day of his death.

During the question and answer sessions at these after dinner speeches Banks would happily explain his astonishing piece of goalkeeping. Likewise, he would gladly spend time talking through the moment with the endless supply of fans who would greet him in restaurants, or in the supermarket, or on the golf course. He would enjoy a smile at his friend Pele's reaction, but otherwise would be matter of fact. Because what was a miracle to fans was to him the result of hard work, training and a willingness to bounce back from mistakes.

He would explain how he spent years mastering positional sense. Despite the marvel in Mexico, Banks did not make that many spectacular saves. He didn't need to. He always managed to be in the right place. But that came thanks to hours of additional practice. In the days before clubs employed a specialist goalkeeping coach he would persuade team mates to stay behind after training and give him extra practice.

He found that this extra work helped him to develop high levels of anticipation. That was not some kind of telepathic gift, but the result of endless hours on the training pitch. So the save for which he is remembered was not just an instinctive and beast like leap. It was also the result of study and anticipation. He knew Pele was a master. He knew he would head the ball firmly and accurately. So he knew where it would end up. In the hardest place for a keeper to reach. Finally, he had arrived in Mexico to find pitches that were rock hard. That meant additional training to work out bounce, and to delay full commitment to dives until the last possible moment. Additional training that Banks had gladly gobbled up.

Gordon Banks, in his quiet, modest way offered advice to young players starting out in the game. To these awe struck kids he would say the following:

- Work hard in training.
- See a mistake as a chance to get better.
- Keep confidence.
- Study the game.
- Enjoy yourself.

Of course, Gordon Banks mostly spoke to would be goalkeepers. But those lessons apply to every child learning the game. They make an outstanding mantra for coaches. And they are especially applicable to players learning about defense.

Every aspect of soccer has team play at its core, but none more so than defensive work. Strikers must know how to defend as much as a centre back. Therefore, the drills and skills we look at here are as relevant to the number nine as they are to the number 3.

Pressing

Most players are pretty good if they are given time and space. Most make mistakes when they are under pressure. Therefore pressing is a growing and essential part of the game. Traditionally, strikers and number tens would make a gentle jog towards and defender in possession, then wait as their opponent's attack developed, leaving it to the midfield and defense to win back possession.

However, teaching young players to press as a team will improve their communication, their understanding of each other's game, their fitness and their involvement of the game. And the more they are involved, the more fun they will derive from the sport.

Defensive Drill: The High Press

This drill involves a full pitch and full teams, and is a conditioned match play situation. The ball begins at the back with a keeper or full back of the non-pressing team. When the transition stage is reached, or play breaks down, the drill restarts. The coach should be prepared to stop the drill regularly, ensuring that players remain in the position they are in, to point out positional strengths and weaknesses. The objectives of the pressing team are:

- Close down space.

- Pressure the player on the ball.

- Make the next pass as difficult as possible.

- Use their growing knowledge of the game to anticipate where the next pass will go. The best teams will be able to work out two or three passes ahead. There are similarities between soccer and chess.

- When the ball is won, move into transition as quickly as possible (we will not focus on this during the drill, but playing through that stage will make the practice more realistic.)

Key Skills:

- Every player must KNOW and PERFORM their role. Note: teams that play the high press are vulnerable if a player does not do their job, since there is space in behind the defense.

- Pressing players close down opponents, approaching them sideways to the ball, and trying to force their opponents onto their weaker foot.

- Opponents will have a spare player, because the pressing team must also keep a cover player. However, teamwork and communication ensures that this player is always the hardest to reach with a pass.

- Pressing is fluid, with the best placed player closing down, marking or covering.

With the high press, it is important to have a fast back line. They will be further up the pitch, which leaves space behind them.

Man Marking

This is a part of the defensive side of the game that is beginning to disappear, at least at higher professional level. And the youth structure should reflect the best practice of the game in its most developed form. Nowadays, man marking will tend only to be used at set pieces. Instead, if a player is to be 'man marked' in open play, it will be the nearest player who is designated to close them down.

The reason for this is a positive one. Offensively, teams are more effective if every player can contribute. So although the central midfielder might well be the best passer, the Number 10 the most creative player, the winger the quickest and the centre forward the one with the best intuition when it comes to goal scoring, every player is expected to be able to contribute. The days of the 'stopper' have come to pass. Something for which referees, spectators and the ankles of talented ball players are eternally grateful.

The negative of this fluid pressing over man marking approach to defense is that players are more regularly drawn out of position. This means that covering for team mates and being aware of space becomes more important. Of course, it is fine to be out of position when attacking, but not when defending. This is why the transition aspect of the game has become so central.

However, when man marking is the system to be used by a team, there are certain techniques a defensive player should be looking to use...

Key Skills of Man Marking:

- Stand close to the opponent being marked.
- Stand goal side – i.e. between the attacker and the goal.
- Position the body at 45 degrees to the ball to enable fast movement.
- Keep on your toes.
- Ensure that you can see your opponent and the ball. If the opponent gets behind you then you cannot see their movement, and that can give a good striker the opportunity to score.

Defensive Drill: Man Marking from Set Plays.

Set up various set plays. Free kicks, throw ins, corners. With younger players, it may be best for the coach to make the set play. Again, for accuracy in can be effective for the coach to throw the ball in underarm. Check the position of defenders, and play out the set play. Discuss the play at the end and get defenders to identify what has worked and what should be improved. This kind of discussion is very important for young players. Verbalising their thoughts helps concepts to be understood and to stick in their heads.

Top Tip: Sometimes coaches, as well meaning as we are, get confused between the terms 'discussion' and 'lecture'. A discussion involves everyone, and gives all a chance to input and clarify their thinking. A lecture involves talking for the coach (or teacher) and sleeping for everybody else.

Zonal Marking

With zonal marking, each player has an area of the pitch for which they are responsible. Communication and cover are vital when players are drawn out of their zones, either to support a team mate, or because they have joined an attack.

Zonal marking improves with practice. There is nothing surprising in that. Use match play situations to identify defensive strengths and weaknesses. Coaches should be prepared to stop practice games regularly to allow players to review their zonal positioning.

Zonal marking is often used with corners. Here, defenders stand along the six yard box, each with an area for which they are responsible. This has the benefit of all parts of the penalty area being covered. In contrast, with man marking, gaps appear since the defensive focus is the opponent rather than the zone. However, with zonal marking, players tend to be stationary and so react less well to opponent's movement.

Research suggests that the best way of defending corners is to crowd the box. The opponent's best headers of the ball are man marked, while zonal defense is also used.

Top Tip: There are very few goals scored from corners in the professional game. Even less when kids are playing. A coach's time is probably better used on any other aspect of the game than coaching corners. Instead, take a short corner if possible, if not lift it into the box and see what materialises. Just remember that having a corner can leave a side vulnerable to a quick counter attack.

Shot Blocking

Defenders have to be brave. Closing down shots is a vital part of their role. The skill of this is a mixture of mental strength and anticipation. In shot blocking, it is important to stay upright and close down rather than dive at the shooter's feet. Once a defender is on the ground, they can easily be beaten, and going to the deck should really be very much a last resort. Approach the shooter at 45 degrees, make the body (not the arms) as big as possible, bend the knees and stay loose and flexible.

At the professional level, defenders will often tuck their arms behind their backs to avoid giving away a penalty. This is poor technique, especially for children, as balance is affected. Having the arms in a natural position should not be a problem. If a referee gives a penalty when the ball hits the arm in this situation, they are not a good referee and will be making plenty of other errors during the game.

We would not advocate specific drills for shot blocking. Instead, we would reward attempts with praise to reinforce their worth. Shot blocking can hurt, and if children block repeatedly during a drill, their confidence will erode and they will hesitate in the heat of a match situation.

One On One Defending.

If shot blocking is not an area of the game that will benefit from specific drills, then one on one defending certainly is.

If defense is mostly a team activity, then one on one defending is the chance for the defender to show their own special skills. Technique is important. When working to improve one on one defending, the following techniques should be stressed.

- Approach at 45 degrees to the player to allow quick changes of direction.
- Stay lightly on the toes, with knees bent.
- Watch the ball, not the player. It is the ball that is important.
- Stay on feet until the player has lost close control of the ball.
- Try to drive the player onto their weaker foot by positioning the body with more space on that weaker side.
- If you are going to be beaten, it should be on the outside, not inside, as this presents the least danger to the goal. Therefore, attacking players should generally be shepherded away from goal.

- Do not commit to the tackle too early. Certainly, this is necessary if the striker is in a position to shoot, but by harrying and jockeying, the attacker will be slowed down, and that allows support to arrive.

Defensive Drill: One On One

This drill requires a half pitch. There are two v two players, with a goalkeeper.

Attacker one starts with the ball wide. He or she attacks defender one by running at them.

Attacker two is slightly in front of defender two. This player makes a run, the defender is not allowed to move until the striker has moved. Therefore, defenders are practising defending from in front of the player, and behind them. The attackers attempt to score or get a shot on goal. The defenders attempt to stop this.

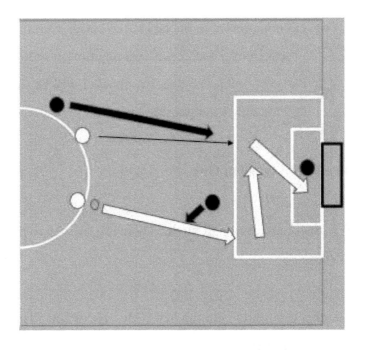

Coaches might have to work a little to persuade their young players of this, but defending can be fun. Acclaim is less frequent than perhaps for a striker, but still as satisfying. Defense is the unsung part of soccer but, as Gordon Banks would say, working hard, training hard, being brave and enjoying the game will help to turn young players into find defenders.

Let us help our young players learn that glory can take many forms!

Learn Soccer by Watching TV

Playing soccer is so much fun that it is little surprise that it is the world's most popular team sport. It is a sport that can be played with almost no equipment. Something to kick (a ball being best!), and two jumpers for goal posts.

At the same time, in its organised form it is highly technical and complex. Scoring in soccer is relatively rare. That is important to the game. At various times, there have been suggestions of making goals bigger to increase the conversion rates of shots. But the intense thrill of scoring is truly enhanced because it does not happen that often.

Other reasons that make soccer a great spectator sport are basic: the ball is large enough to see easily, the pitch big enough to allow large crowds.

But soccer is best when players have passion. Passion when they play…but also about the game in general. That means having a team to support. There is a joy watching your local team, at whatever standard they play, or a friend's team. Even better is to support a professional side. However, in the US that is not as easy as in many other parts of the world, because of the size of he country and the relatively few top professional clubs.

Live in Los Angeles and LA Galaxy is the only fully professional option. Live in London and young fans can go to see Arsenal, Chelsea, West Ham United, Charlton Athletic, Queens Park Rangers, Barnet, Crystal Palace, Fulham, Tottenham Hotspurs and so on.

But young kids can follow European teams, and watch them regularly on TV. There are a lot of influences that turn a youngster into a fan, and success is one of them. Here is a brief run down of some of the top European teams. Our aim in showing these is to develop children's love of the game. Yes, they learn most by playing, but supporting a team means that (certainly by the time they reach nine or ten) they will enjoy watching their side on TV. Then they learn from watching the best, from studying the post-match analysis of experts, from seeing their own favourite players performing. That can all only help their love of the game.

Spain: Two teams dominate here. Barcelona and Real Madrid. Probably the two most successful teams in Europe, their domination is only distantly challenged by one other, Atletico Madrid.

Germany: Again, at the moment German football is dominated by two teams. These are Bayern Munich, with their established track record of success. But currently the new kids on the block, Dortmund, are out on top.

France: Sadly, while French football is on high at national level – they won the World Cup in 2018, at club level it is a non-competitive one horse race. PSG have all the money, and so win all the trophies.

Italy: If French football is on a high, Italian is struggling a little. But there is plenty of competition at league level. The Milan teams, AC and Inter, are traditional strong holds. Roma are on a high. Juventus are the strongest Italian team at the moment.

England: Many believe the English Premier League to be the most competitive, with any of six teams often sharing cup and league success. Most matches are also available on TV. The top teams are the Manchester clubs, United and City, Liverpool, and three London sides: Arsenal, Tottenham Hotspurs and Chelsea.

Once young players have their teams, watching them on TV can be a really useful way of helping them to understand the game. Parents and coaches can ease these young players towards a focus on the many aspects of the game. Encourage them to study their favourite team, and their favourite players. Watching masters can only help their understanding of the techniques of the game. Players such as Virgil Van Dyke in defense, Mesut Ozil in midfield, Lionel Messi or Ronaldo up front, and especially the newest star of the game, Kylian Mbappe, must be positive for young players' development.

The following areas are ones where TV can provide both entertainment and a great learning experience. They are parts of the game that are often picked up on during post-match analysis but if this is unavailable, or unsuitable for what we are trying to achieve, the pause and replay buttons can give help us to use the coverage to our advantage. Some coverage has 'player cam' which tracks a particular player. This can be useful in showing young players have hard their professional heroes work during a game. We have offered a tip or focal point for each aspect but, of course, these will vary depending on the interests and needs of the young players, plus their attitude to studying the game.

We should never lose sight of the fact that soccer should be fun!

Movement: Compare the different movements between offense and defense. Successful movement will see attacking sides getting players wide, with midfielders and number 10s attempting to get in the spaces between lines of defense. Centre-forwards will be trying to split the centre halves, creating gaps to be exploited by their midfield.

By contrast, in defences will try hard to keep a back four in a line, and probably five across midfield. Players will move out of their position to press, with team mates shuffling across to cover for them.

In a previous chapter, we likened soccer to a game of chess. Watching movement we see the constant tactical battle to find space on one side, and deny it on the other. This is fascinating to adults, but to kids who would rather be playing it is a dish best served in small portions.

First Touch and Protecting the Ball: This is useful part of the game to watch on TV for a couple of reasons. Mostly, we can see those skills kids practise in training being put into action in a top level, professional game. We can also show kids that even the best players sometimes get it wrong. That is a useful lesson for helping to reinforce resilience.

Body Position (defending and receiving the pass): A difference young players might notice here is how much more physical the game is at the adult level. A lot of the contact seen on TV would be penalised in a junior match. Helping kids to find a happy balance between physicality and fairness is always difficult, but the TV can offer one extreme to young players.

Passing: A coach can collect together a selection of close ups of players passing the ball, and use these as a coaching tool for a drill on passing.

Decision Making: Coaches can put together clips, or freeze live matches or highlights, and get young players to debate the decisions players make, which ones are good and which misjudged. The clips can then be played on and the results of decision making discussed.

Team Formation: Overhead angles can offer a great view on how a team is set up, better even than can be seen from high up in a stadium. Once more, coaches can put together their own clips and create a quiz in which the team look at a formation and discuss the set up the professional coach has used. This can make a great activity at an end of season get together, or as a way to break up a lengthy pre-season training session where the players need the occasional rest from physical work.

Team Press: The hardest part about getting young players to press as a team is installing in the players the understanding that each of them has a vital role to play. This extends not just to the player closing down an opponent, but the full back on the opposite side of the pitch who is ensuring that, in two passes time, his winger is not going to find himself in a dangerous amount of space. Watching how professional teams operate the high press can help with this understanding. Get young players to watch their equivalent in the professional teams on show.

Transition: The speed of transition, movement of players and one touch passing makes this one of the most exciting parts of the game. Simply watching for this thrilling change in pace in a game provides huge entertainment. When they are watching great play, children are engaged, and when they are engaged, they are learning.

What we are saying is that the coach should let the transition stage play out on TV matches. Perhaps he or she might return to discuss individual players' roles later, but avoids disrupting the flow of the game as it happens.

Offensive plays: It is great fun to see drills we have worked on in our own training sessions being used at the highest level of the game. If it is great for us, as coaches and adults, then it is even more exciting for children.

Defensive Plays: Ditto as above.

Game Management: We have included this for a negative reason. Game management is really a euphemism. It is a way professionals and pundits explain away negative play which is designed to hold on to an advantage. We want our young players to enjoy the sport for what it should be, and not just focus on winning a game.

Why settle for 2-1, when the result could be 4-3?

Dribbling Skills

Dribbling is one of the most thrilling aspects of the game. There is something indescribably impressive about watching a quick winger dropping their shoulder, knocking the ball and speeding past a full back, leaving the defender stumbling in treacle.

We looked earlier at how general dribbling skills can be developed as a part of the warm up to a training session. In this chapter we will look in much more detail at specific drills and techniques which can help players to improve their dribbling skills and techniques.

Children love to dribble. The challenge is often to get them to pass, not getting the ball glued to their feet. So the coach is off to a positive start. The next stage is to use that natural enthusiasm which oozes from every pore of young soccer players, and shape it into the skills which will stand them in good stead throughout their playing career.

Dribbling Drill: Tagging Game

This drill is great way to get children using the key skills of dribbling; close control, using both feet, inside and outside of those feet and, vitally, keeping their heads up.

It is a fun game, ideal for warm ups, quick to set in place and one which involves lots of action: in other words, perfect for young players.

The coach marks out a large grid – the centre circle or a penalty box works just as well. The entire team takes part. The players each have a ball and must dribble in the box without going out. One player wears a bib and this is the 'Tagger'. Her aim is to touch, or tag, one of the other players. This can only be done while the tagger has their own ball under control.

The coach supervises action, and reminds players constantly to keep their heads up, to use both feet and also both the inside and outside of these.

Dribbling Drill: Making Decisions

Decision making is always important for players who are dribbling. When to pass? Should I shoot? Do I take on another player? Not only are these challenging decisions when the ball is at their feet and they have time to consider the options, but when they have to be made running at speed, the level of difficulty increases all the time.

And if the wrong decision is made, then all that good dribbling work can be wasted. How many times have we seen a skilled winger gradually disappear out of a team because their final decision is poor?

This drill involves three teams, each with three players. One of the players is nominated as a goalkeeper, and this player can be rotated. Mark out a rough triangle with sides of 20m. One cone per corner is fine, and coaches should not worry too much about balls running out of play. A small goal is placed along each side.

The drill develops neatly. Stage one is a simple attacker v goalkeeper dribble. Each team dribbles the ball and tries to score into the goal on their left. This can be swapped to the goal on their right as the coach wishes. It is a continuous activity with the second player in each team starting once his or her team has taken their shot at goal.

After a couple of rounds of this, a defender is added. So the team of three now has a defender, a dribbler and a keeper. In this 1 v 1 stage scoring is more difficult.

The main part of the drill is a simultaneous 3 x 3 x 3 match, with all three goals in use. Teams can score in any goal, except their own. As can be imagined, the drill now becomes highly action packed, with play moving in all directions. The confusion of a real match is thus recreated. Also, players are constantly making decisions. When to attack? When to defend? Pass or dribble?

This excellent drill can be returned to as players develop their individual skills. There is the challenge for the coach as to whether they introduce individual skills before the tactical skills developed in this drill.

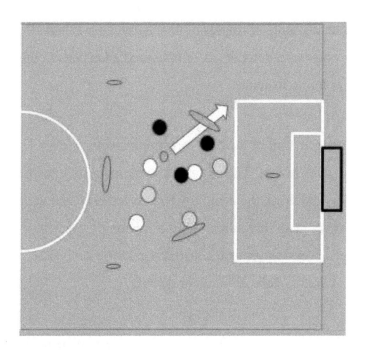

Normally, we would advocate practising the technical skill prior to the tactical one. Dribbling is perhaps the only exception to this rule. This is because it is something young players do naturally. Indeed, they can over dribble. Therefore, by getting them to think about what they will actually achieve with their dribbling becomes important. Make the correct decision and their success rate will increase, and with that so will their confidence. As a result, they will be prepared to experiment more and thus develop personal dribbling skills.

Dribbling Drill: Moving Inside

Wing play is not just about dribbling wide and crossing. Indeed, many teams now look to use a predominantly right footed player on the left hand side of the pitch, and vice versa. On the one hand, this can help defenders since they can work out that the player is likely to cut inside onto their stronger foot before passing or crossing. However, it cutting inside allows dribblers to get into shooting positions.

The phenomenal French striker, Thierry Henry, was a real specialist a driving in from the left hand side of the pitch, cutting in and onto his right foot, then opening his body to side foot the ball home into the far corner. (Of course, being two footed makes the player even more of a threat!)

Show your young players clips of his goals, they offer a real insight into the way a striker can use this skill to amazing effect.

Cutting inside also creates space for a full back or wing back to get outside the dribbler, posing a double problem for the defender. Do they try to track the dribbler, or do they try to cover the overlapping player? That momentary pause while a decision is made is frequently enough for the dribbling striker to get away his pass or shot.

This drill involves a range of options, and so decision making is crucial. It is a rondo style drill, with three attackers against one defender and a goalkeeper.

Top Tip: Set up straight forward dribbling exercises, such as dribble, cut inside and shoot, to use every session. They are quick to organise, simple to explain and over the course of a season young players will become much stronger at dribbling.

Player one is the dribbler. He or she dribbles and cuts inside. Player two is the full back. This player makes a run down the outside of the winger, to provide an option for the pass. Player three is a striker. He or she runs laterally (to simulate staying onside, and cuts at 45 degrees to either receive the pass for a shot, or to take the defender away to create space for the dribbler. The defender attempts to anticipate the movement of the ball and defend against it.

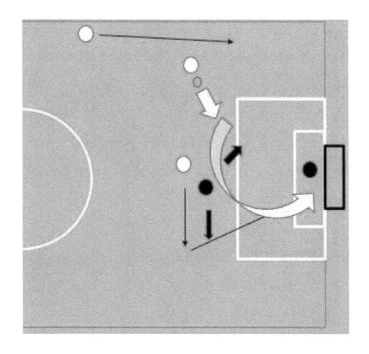

The coach here should be encouraging the team to drive forward at speed; space for a dribble like this often comes in transition, and so the attack needs to be completed swiftly (in a match) before the defense can reorganise. The coach should encourage running off the ball, communication and best decision making for the player in possession.

Dribbling Against the Keeper

Strikers will find themselves in 1 v 1 situations with the keeper. They should be encouraged to make their minds up quickly, and attack at speed. If a defensive player is in pursuit, the attacker needs to cut across this player to place their body between defender and ball.

This makes a tackle very difficult. In the adult game, if the defender gets the tackle wrong, he faces giving away a penalty and, depending on the level and seriousness of the match, receiving a red card.

The red card is unlikely to happen at youth level, unless the game is at the highest standard for the age group, but it is still important to teach youngsters the best way to play.

The striker has a number of options when running at the keeper. The speed at which he is moving, the level of control on the ball, position of the keeper and the angle of approach all have to be taken into account in order for the striker to make the best decision.

We suggest practising all options, so players feel confident with whichever route they choose.

Shooting Early: The goalkeeper will be anxious to narrow the angles for the striker as quickly as possible. It can be effective to shoot before the goalie has time to do this. The advantages of this early shot are:

- The striker is under less pressure.
- The goalkeeper is not set to save the shot.

However, the shot is coming from further out, which gives a wider margin for error.

Shooting From Closer to the Keeper: A good goalkeeper will be looking to make the angle into which a shot will go into the net as small as possible, while keeping themselves as big a possible. A striker who is confident and knows that they are going to do will usually score in a 1 v 1; one who is indecisive will usually miss, or have their shot saved. The goalkeeper is therefore aiming to maximise that indecisiveness.

A striker can negate this by shooting when they, themselves, feel in the best position. In drills encourage strikers to hit shots firmly with the instep. The ball should be directed close to the keeper, but wide enough so that it cannot be saved with the feet. Often, a firm, low shot will travel under the keeper as they try to make themselves as big as possible.

Advantages and disadvantages of this approach:

- It should be easy to hit the target.
- But the keeper is well set and has closed down the angles.

Nevertheless, this tends to be the approach strikers use most of the time we can encourage kids to follow the example of better players and look to this method as their normal approach. That is not to say that they should not adapt when circumstances dictate. Therefore, all methods should be practised in drills.

Chipping the Keeper: Very spectacular; and very hard to achieve. The aim here is for the striker to drop their shoulder, or 'give the eyes' to make the keeper commit to their dive. As they go down, the striker leans slightly backwards and stabs under the ball with his foot, to lift it.

While this is the most spectacular way of finishing a 1 v 1 with a keeper, and is highly satisfying when it works, it carries risks.

- Controlling direction and height is difficult, because the ball is chipped with the toes.
- If the keeper does not 'buy the dummy' and stays tall, he will easily stop the shot.

Again, the use of the dummy can help to commit the keeper. The striker wants them to go to ground early so that they can be rounded. A good way to practise is to get young strikers to dummy to the inside of their foot, and drag it wide the opposite way with the outside of the same foot. This way, the keeper is likely to dive the wrong way.

Most keepers would prefer that their striker attempts to go round them, and will back themselves to prevent this. That in itself is a good reason for using this method sparingly. However, because these days strikers tend to shoot on 1 v 1 situations, there is a surprise value when the man or woman approaching decides to attempt to go round the advancing keeper.

It is particularly effective if the keeper tries to close down too quickly, as they will be off balance when the ball changes direction.

There are advantages and disadvantages associated with trying to round the keeper. On the plus side:

- Unless the keeper gets a good touch on the ball, a goal or penalty is very likely.

- Keepers will expect a shot.

But on the other hand:

- Keepers can go full length to win the ball, so it may have to be knocked wide to go past the opponent.
- That can take the ball wide, making the angle for the shot difficult, even though it is into an open goal.
- Because the process is slower than trying a shot, defenders have more chance of getting back to cover.
- Attackers may lose their balance as they change direction at pace.

Nevertheless, whichever approach is used by strikers when they are through on the keeper, it is a drill which they will really enjoy working on during training sessions. It is a win, win, win situation.

Strikers get the chance to dribble (check), shoot (check) and score (double tick). Keepers have the opportunity to be a hero. And who doesn't like that? Especially when they are ten years old!

Mental Exercises Before the Game

Time to get into debating mode with this chapter. Because while there are extremely close ties between adult soccer and the youth or children's game when it comes to skills, fitness and tactics, that is much, much less the case when we consider the mental side of the sport.

In this chapter we will consider the pros and cons of giving kids mental strength guidance and training. We will look at how this can provide life skills when used productively. And how it leads to a narrow, negative outlook when the mental exercises are simply about winning.

Why Mental Strength Exercises Can Be Counter Productive

'I was pleased with the mental strength of my players...' states the coach in the post-match interview. When we hear that kind of statement, we don't need to look at the score to know that the team have had a battle on their hands, maybe a winning one, perhaps a losing one.

Mental exercises are used by coaches and players to help focus the mind. They can include visualisation tasks, positive thinking activities and team building type actions. The primary aim behind mental strength exercises in adult soccer is to improve a winning mentality.

But the extent to which we wish to inculcate that into young players is something about which psychologists and child development experts are raising doubts. A winning attitude is by nature a competitive one. The goal in a competitive situation (which includes going beyond soccer) is to beat an opponent. Until quite recently, this adversarial approach to life was seen as positive. Whether it was in sport, in law, in business, in school or in the family, to be a winner was good and nobody wanted to know a loser. Yet we know now that collaboration is a more effective tool than competition when it comes to personal development. Although we are talking about life in general here, we can draw an analogy with soccer.

A team will be more successful if they play as a unit than if they each compete to be 'the best' member of the team. That can be a tricky lesson for children to learn. Actually, the same can be said for adults.

We are not suggesting that there is anything fundamentally wrong with a winning mentality. But coaches, and parents, should (we argue) consider 'why' a winning mentality is good. They might then come to the conclusion that actually, while it is fine to win, there is a great deal in life that is more important. And playing soccer can really help youngsters to learn that valuable lesson.

The Benefits of Mental Resilience

When we start to consider the wider benefits of mental resilience, and exercises that help to develop these, the world starts to look much less foggy, and the training we will advocate begins to make sense. Because mental strength benefits all aspects of life, not just soccer.

People, including children, with mental resilience think more of themselves. They develop better relationships; they are able to cope better with disappointments and changes to their lives. Physical and mental health improves and, most important of all, people are happier.

If there is a secondary benefit that they do better in their soccer, then that is a bonus coaches will not turn away. We all have a duty to help the young people in our teams. That duty goes beyond parents. It includes the wider family, teachers and sports coaches. Indeed, sport offers great opportunities for young people to develop self-esteem, self believe and offer more to their community.

So our conclusion is that when we play sport for the fun, the physical benefits it offers, the teamwork, collaboration and friendship it brings, then that is sport for good. When we play sport to win at all costs, then using mental strength exercises to further this is a destructive action. We want victory to be a side product of all the good that soccer offers to young players, not the driving force behind their playing of the game.

What Mental Strength Benefits Help Young People Across All Aspects of Their Lives

The following traits are ones that all would surely promote as being beneficial to young and old alike. Simply playing sport brings many of them to young players, provided we get our youngsters on the park for the right reasons.

Specific exercises might enhance these benefits further. Let us consider that mental strength advantages we should be aiming to promote.

Commitment: Training hard in soccer sessions will transfer itself to commitment to school, to hard work and to improving oneself.

Desire: That wish to become a better soccer player can be translated into a wish to improve in all aspects of life. Not just the competitive ones, such as sport or games, but also a desire to improve relationships, or help the wider community. Studies in schools have shown than on many occasions those who participate in sport with a desire to improve, tend to do well in other aspects of academic and social studies, at least in relation to their potential. Interestingly, the same is much less true when soccer players are picked simply because they are good, although their work rate and desire to improve is less impressive. As those of us who have worked with children know, they tend to be the players who, over time, drop out of the sport.

Focus: Good soccer players learn to focus on the task in hand. This allows them to break down the bigger picture of winning a game or scoring a goal into the separate elements that lead to this. For example, winning a tackle, making a pass, working as a team and pushing oneself. Many aspects of life are built around a big picture that is best broken down into its constituent parts. Conversely, young people who find this focusing on specific tasks often struggle and fail in their aims, leading to lower self esteem and less happiness. For example, revising for an exam can seem an overwhelming task, so much so some give up before they start. Those able to break down revision into small, manageable chunks do much better in their tests.

Detail: On the soccer pitch, players need to be at their best physically and mentally in order to become the best players they can be. Children with the motivation to do this often transfer such an attitude to their wider life.

Resilience: So important. Everybody experiences bad times as well as good. Nobody avoids failure all of the time. A resilient person sees a failure as an opportunity to improve; somebody without that resilience sees it as a reason to give up.

Motivation: Soccer helps to develop the ability to set both individual and collective goals. For example, a player may work harder to try to hold on to a 1 – 0 lead, giving a collective benefit. At the same time, they will try to develop their own, for example, dribbling skills, to create more chances for beating an opponent.

Responding To Challenge: Soccer helps youngsters to respond to challenges set by opponents, their own coaches and their team mates. It also helps them to set their own challenges. The ability to achieve these in soccer can be transferred to wider life.

Progress: To glass half empty believers, there is a sense that they are not improving, or progressing. The good coach will reward success, effort and improvement, getting players to reflect on how far they and the team has come on. Once more, that is a life skill.

Determination: Closely linked to resilience and motivation, sports players have that wish to succeed, even when things are going against them.

Leadership: The best leadership is collaborative. It is working with team mates, rather than instructing them what to do. What better way is there to show leadership in this way than in a team game?

Control, Composure and Self-Discipline: Soccer is a team, contact sport run by an objective arbiter. Decisions can sometimes go against a player, but the game helps them to learn to accept this and to continue without allowing them to dwell on the perceived mis-treatment. That way it passes, and does not cast a pall of gloom on other aspects of life.

Flexibility: Soccer requires the individual to challenge themselves, and to react to circumstances. Like life, in fact.

Self-Confidence: The best soccer players are self-confident. They believe that they can benefit others if they work hard and do their best.

137

They are not arrogant, with a false perception of their own worth. Self confidence is, perhaps along with resilience, the most important mental strength that can be helped through playing soccer.

Exercises and Behaviours to Improve Mental Strength

So we can see the enormous mental advantages playing soccer (or indeed, other team sports) can offer to an individual. We can see how those mental strengths translate to wider situations in life, and help young people to cope with the challenges of growing up in today's United States of America.

However, coaches can assist the development of these strengths. Young people do get things wrong and they need encouraging in the right direction. The following simple drills and actions will help to achieve this.

Mental Drill: A Positive Approach

Not really a drill, more a mantra by which a team is run, this exercise is nevertheless crucial in helping the mental strength of players.

Coaches can make an environment that is encouraging and supportive, rather than critical. While most would support this as an obvious move, achieving it can be harder than might seem. Adults are often more competitive than their offspring. Therefore, they find it hard to understand that attitudes or team decisions have longer term goals than securing a short term win.

While the coach might offer only praise and constructive criticism, parents, spectators and the young players themselves might hold a less positive mindset. The coach therefore looks to establish a 'no criticism' mindset. Players do not moan if they fail to receive a pass, or a team mate misses a shot when they perceive themselves to be better placed.

Parents praise and support rather than coach and criticise. Perhaps even a code of conduct can be written for parents to sign before committing their child to the team. As coaches we love sport, we would not be involved if we did not. Therefore, we love competition and hence we love winning. Putting our own motivations lower down the list of priorities than the well being and long term development of our players might occasionally be hard, but should always be our goal.

Mental Drill: Positive Re-enforcement

Hold a post-match or after practice discussion in which every person contributes with a positive comment about a team mate's performance. Or, each player draws a name from a hat, and must finish the session by saying something positive about the team mate they have drawn.

Mental Drill: Visualisation

We want our sessions to be fun. To kids usually the most fun happens when they have their game. Or, at least they think it does. Spend five minutes before a session getting players to visualise the skills they are about to practice in a game situation.

Mental Drill: Improving Communication – The Architect Game

The following drill is excellent for building communication skills. It is a non-soccer drill, so offers a nice variety in a sports based session. Organise sets of different coloured and sized Lego pieces, or other children's building blocks. Duplicate the set. Each team has two sets, the original and the duplicate.

Divide the group into teams of four. The team should be placed at least 50 metres apart, and the builder should not be able to see the architect or hear the first communicator. Each member then has a specific role.

The Architect – takes one set of bricks and builds his shape.

The First Communicator – takes description of the shape to the...

Second Communicator – who passes the instruction on to the...

Builder – who tries to recreate the shape with the duplicate set of bricks.

Mental Drill: Collaborative Activity – Team Juggling

This fun event helps with development of soccer close control skills as well as teamwork. Divide the squad into teams of about five or six. One ball per group. Starting with an underarm throw, players juggle the ball without it hitting the ground for as many touches as possible.

They can use any part of the body allowed in soccer. Players can touch the ball twice before passing it on, but this only counts as one touch. They continue until the ball hits the floor. Each group tries to improve their score.

Players will learn that they need to communicate – if two players go for the same ball control is lost. They will discover that working as a team they do better. For example, closing in on each other when the ball starts to go out of control, spreading out when it is under control to give them more time.

This exercise works best if it is *not* a competition between groups. With that, players' focus turns to beating opponents rather than improving themselves. After all, the ultimate goal in any activity is surely not to win, but to be the best you can be?

Fun Games

We can practice soccer skills in the context of fun games. While kids will most want to play soccer, they enjoy other activities. Give them catching practice using a small ball. Play soccer tennis over a line. Play soccer baseball.

Here, the pitcher passes the ball along the ground. The hitter kicks the ball as far as he or she can. The fielders try to catch the ball, or pass it back to a post. Fun is the emphasis here.

Mental Drill: Soccer Charades

Another fun, team building mental exercise. The coach writes the name of soccer related ideas on sheets of paper. For example, the names of players, teams, stadia, competitions or aspects of the game, such as 'shooting'. The person on must act out the term on their sheet *without* miming any soccer related movement. And the other players should guess the word.

The enjoyment players get transfers to the session as a whole. It also helps to develop an understanding of the game, and an interest in it. After all, if their imagination is caught, youngsters will want to find out more about the player they have just impersonated, or the stadium they have just described.

A Chapter for Parents

How can parents help their kids to get the most out of their soccer? Hopefully, the points we have stressed in the book are ones into which parents can buy.

Fundamentally, our position is that soccer for young people is about developing skills that will serve them well throughout their life in the game. It is about gaining the joy that comes from supporting a team, and holding an interest in the fan side of the game.

Being a soccer player, we argue, prepares the young participant for life. The mental strength the game can give transfers itself to many other aspects of meeting the challenges of living in the modern world.

That the camaraderie, friendship and collaboration that takes place on the soccer field, the club house and, perhaps most of all, the training park help to make life even better than it already is. But most of all, we have emphasised that joining a soccer team should be fun.

The Benefits for Parents

Of course, we sign our kids up because they want to play. We realise that we are committing ourselves to muddy cars and dirty boots for the foreseeable future. Our lives as taxi drivers for our kids gets a little more frantic, if that is possible. But we do so with pleasures, but it makes our kids happy.

But we can be a little selfish. We will get benefits of our own from becoming a soccer mom or dad. Consider the following:

- We get the pleasure of watching our kids do something they enjoy. Watching sport is interesting in its own right. When we have a personal interest in the match, this becomes even more the case.
- We get to mix with a community who share interests with us. Chatting on the side line, having a beer in the bar – these are very enjoyable past times. At no other time do we want our kids to get changed more slowly, or spend longer packing away their boots.
- We know our kids are in a safe environment, undertaking useful exercise.

But pleasures come with responsibilities, and being a soccer parent does have its challenges. They are well worth facing, because the benefits far outweigh them, but for new soccer parents it is best to have an idea of some of the gentle waves in the distance on the otherwise perfectly calm sea of sporting joy.

Controlling Our Own Competitive Spirits

There is a well known ex soccer player, with a global reputation, who is now involved in sports presenting. He held the impressive achievement of never being sent off, and never being booked. Such an achievement reflects well on his fairness and his sportsmanship. His role model reputation allied to presenting TV programmes to millions around the world gives him the opportunity to share his views on a wide range of topics. It is probably best not to name this personality, because we are about to be a little critical of one of his views.

A couple of years ago, after watching his own kids playing soccer, he posted a series of tweets expressing disgust at parents on the side lines of matches. He has a point, there's no question there, but has probably overstated it.

There are some parents who undoubtedly do let themselves down. Which almost certainly results in the total embarrassment of their offspring. These are parents who know more than the coach (perhaps they do, but it is not their job to show it). They are critical of the referee's performance. We all make mistakes. Even referees. But these parents know that they are faultless themselves (they are being ironic when commenting on their own small failings) and expect others to live up to their standards. They berate the opposition – which is just plain rude. They shout at their own child, damaging his confidence, her self-esteem. Perhaps worst of all, they criticise their own side, especially when a team mate has failed to pass to their own kid.

Probably, in all other aspects of their lives, these are thoroughly decent people, kind hearted and supportive. (Actually, we are just saying that. Many of these kind are as bullying in their wider lives as they are on the side lines. But not all. There is hope for some. And we don't know who might be reading this book). But something takes them over, like an evil spirit that is mostly kept in check, when they reach the sports field. That demon is their own over competitive nature. It blinds them to reality; it takes away the inhibitions that would normally never see them berate an unknown child or complete stranger. It embarrasses them in every eye except for their own.

147

Our un-named sporting icon went too far. He suggested that parents should do no more than clap at a game. That the overwhelming majority did not know how to behave. He is wrong. Mostly. But, as hard as it is to say, if we are the parent – mom or, more commonly, dad who is a parental hooligan, then we need to recognise that and do something about it. We owe it to the unpaid coach who gives his or her time willingly; to the referee without whom the game couldn't take place. We owe it to the players, and to our own child.

Lecture over. Phew. But it had to be said.

Defining Goals and Targets

We have established that winning is a pleasant side effect of commitment, practice, teamwork, resilience, skill and so forth. Therefore, when we set goals with our kids, these will be the aspects of soccer – sport – life – that we promote.

Goals in soccer do not vary a lot from goals in life. The best ones are small and achievable, rather than some distant, hazy blur on the horizon. For example, passing with a weaker foot is specific; getting into the regional Under 15 team when you are 8 is not.

Children can find that sort of specific target hard to come up with; training them to think that way will help them to set realistic goals in life, not just soccer.

Goals should be measurable. So, 'I'm going to play well,' is hard to judge. The definition 'well' needs a context to be judged against. However, 'I will pass the ball accurately three quarters of the time' is easy to keep a track on.

Also, they should be attainable. As appealing as it is for a kid to want to play for his or her country, it doesn't often happen. That is a dream, not a goal. It is fine to have dreams. But we don't measure the success of them. An attainable goal would be for a player to work hard on their fitness so that they can still make box to box runs in the last ten minutes of a game.

Of course, a goal needs to be relevant. Again, younger kids often find it difficult to structure their thinking with relevance. 'I will get a shirt with MESSI on the back' is a goal, and could be achieved. It won't do a lot for that child's soccer skills, though.

Finally, goals need to have an end point. 'I will have made ten key passes in matches by Christmas' is a measurable goal.

Specific

Measurable

Attainable

Relevant

Time Bound

Which are, we can see, SMART goals. Much better to have a SMART goal than a stupid ones. Helping our kids to set themselves smart goals for soccer, something for which they are highly motivated, will give them a handy leg up towards setting goals for their studies and for other parts of life that are, possibly, even more important than soccer. (If such a thing is possible).

Useful Note: The Great Bill Shankly once said: 'Some people believe football is a matter of life and death. I am very, very disappointed with that attitude. I can assure you it is far more important that life or death.'

Expectations

Have you ever watched a game of rugby union? As a sport, it is growing in the US and is popular in Canada, although it remains most popular in the Eastern Hemisphere, especially the Antipodean region and northern Europe.

It's a complicated game, but very enjoyable. If you do get the opportunity to search the cable channels and find a match it will be well worth the time and effort. Have a listen when a penalty is given and a player is in trouble. Answering back? Never. In fact, watching a hairy brute nod their head like a naughty school boy, while meekly saying 'Yes sir' to the ear wagging they are getting from the man with the whistle.

Not something we see in soccer, and that's a shame.

But in coaching our kids towards respect and acceptance of a decision, we are spreading good sportsmanship about. There's a lot to be said for that.

The Importance of Practice

151

It's not usually difficult to get kids up for matches, weekly training sessions can be a different matter. Having said that, a good coach will make sessions fun and there will be a happy spirit in the club. The old ways of Tom Sawyer values, with coaches who terrified the youngsters under their care are long gone.

Certainly, there are those who bemoan the lack of toughness such regimes used to instil. But they tend to be the sorts who responded well to that kind of coaching by bullying, and ended up successful. For every success story like theirs, there are countless other players who gave the game up because the pressure became too great, or the sessions too negative.

Having said that, there will be times when other attractions appeal more than ninety minutes of chilly training. Parents have a tough but necessary role here of ensuring their kids honour their commitments. That loyalty is a life skill which will stand them in good stead when they enter the adult world.

Dealing With Failure and Disappointment

We are talking about our kids' failure and disappointment here, not that of parents! Kids are tough cookies. Knocked out in the semi finals of a big tournament, losing the third place play off on penalties. It doesn't get worse than that. Players may be down for a bit. Sometimes, with young sides in particular, there might even be a few tears.

But ten minutes later they will be bouncing about as normal. The back of the bus on the long road home will be as noisy as ever, shrill voices having moved on. The coach might be ruing lost opportunities and missed chances, but it is unlikely that his team will. Because we have the joy of coaching kids – and the young are very, very good at keeping matters in perspective.

That is right. Despite the words of Bill Shankly, soccer is not more important than life and death. It is fun. It is sport played for the enjoyment running and shooting and being with team mates brings.

So there should not really be a case of dealing with failure and disappointment. Where there is, in all probability those emotions have been learned from coaches or parents themselves.

Instead, failure can be seen as the next step towards success, disappointment as an opportunity to see the next good times feel even better. In other words, a positive outlook breeds positivity. Another lesson for life.

Conclusion

Introducing soccer to kids is a worthwhile and rewarding job. We may be a coach, giving up our time and energy to give a group of youngsters the chance to play a sport that will get them fit, prepare them for life and offer them a huge amount of fun. Or a parent, taking our little ones for a kick around in the park, making sure their boots and shin pads are clean and ready to go, and ferrying car fulls of energetic youngsters across the State. Perhaps we are a teacher, looking to give our classes a chance to play some soccer.

Either way, the time we invest will be more than rewarded. In this book we have offered coaching tips and drills on important aspects of soccer. Offense, defense, passing and dribbling. These skill sessions are tailor made for young players, taking into account their physical and emotional development.

We have looked at how TV can help young players by exposing them to the best players and greatest experts in the world. How it can promote enthusiasm by bringing their favorite team or player to their home. TV can bring the excitement of the game played at the highest level to young supporters and participants, not just through matches but also the expert analysis of performances after the game.

Video clips on sites such as You Tube can also inspire and educate young players.

We have looked at the important role of parents, of recognizing the importance of supporting our kids without playing out our own dreams through their efforts.

Most of all we have seen that getting our youngsters involved in soccer teaches them lessons and disciplines that go way beyond the touchlines of a soccer pitch. These are skills and competences that will help them to develop and maintain great relationships, as well as do well in their studies and work life as they get older.

We have looked at the importance of understanding how children develop emotionally and physically, and how these inform the drills we do and the way we deal with growing kids. Most of all, we have tried to stress the importance of making soccer fun. By its nature, the sport is hugely enjoyable to watch, and even more so to play. Because of the simplicity of the game, it is perfectly suited to young people.

The round ball form of football is gaining popularity in the US for both boys and girls. Let's hope we can contribute to that growth, and add another arm to the sporting life of the country, and its most important people – the young.

The end… almost!

Reviews are not easy to come by.

As an independent author with a tiny marketing budget, I rely on readers, like you, to leave a short review on Amazon.

Even if it's just a sentence or two!

So if you enjoyed the book, please browse to the product page and leave a review as shown below:

I am very appreciative for your review as it truly makes a difference.

Thank you from the bottom of my heart for purchasing this book and reading it to the end.

CPSIA information can be obtained
at www.ICGtesting.com
Printed in the USA
BVHW032153121222
654097BV00024B/656